DUKE UNIVERSITY PRESS · SOCIOLOGICAL SERIES

HOWARD E. JENSEN, CONSULTING EDITOR

Spanish-Speaking Groups
in the United States

John H. Burma:

SPANISH-SPEAKING GROUPS
IN THE UNITED STATES

Duke University Press

1954

Second printing, 1961

PRINTED AND BOUND IN THE UNITED STATES OF AMERICA
BY BOOK CRAFTSMEN ASSOCIATES, INC., NEW YORK

EDITORIAL NOTE

Among the ethnic minorities in the United States who claim some language other than English as their mother tongue, only the Spanish-speaking groups are of increasing importance, both relatively and in terms of absolute numbers. Since the passage of the numerically restrictive Quota Act of 1921 the total foreign-speaking population has steadily declined, while the quota-free Spanish-speaking peoples, especially those of Mexican nativity, have continued to increase. According to the Census of 1940, our 1,861,400 Spanish-speaking residents were exceeded among those reporting an alien mother tongue only by the Germans (4,949,780), the Italians (3,766,820), and the Poles (2,416,320). While comparable data for 1950 are not yet available, the tides of migration indicate a continued increase of our Spanish-speaking population, and a decline of considerable proportions in other linguistic groups.

These Spanish-speaking minorities are in many ways unique among the migrant peoples who have contributed of their blood and their culture to the building of America. None other has combined so great a linguistic unity and so large a common core of culture with so great a variety of racial stocks and historical backgrounds. The Spanish Americans, or Hispanos, concentrated in the uplands of

North Central Mexico and Southern Colorado, constitute a cultural island of colonial Spain surviving behind its barriers of geographical isolation into the twentieth century, while the predominantly Indian Mexicans and the predominantly Malay Filipinos present striking contrasts of physical traits and historical backgrounds to the Hispanos, to each other, and to the Puerto Ricans, among whom a Negroid element constitutes more than a third of the population of their commonwealth. This diversity of racial composition and social and political history presents so wide a variety of problems of adjustment, acculturation, and assimilation that no author has heretofore attempted to treat the salient facts within the covers of a single volume, but the unity of language and culture are nevertheless so great as to lead Professor Burma to undertake the task.

The Mexicans, who comprise by far the largest of the groups here studied, present certain other features unique in the history of human migration. Never before have two cultures representing such striking contrasts in technological development confronted one another across a practically unguarded and for the most part sparsely settled border more than two thousand miles in extent. A plethora of workers eager for wages easily accessible to prospective employers avid for profits is a common occurrence in economic and social history, and has always provided a situation ripe for exploitation. But never has such a situation existed under geographical and political conditions fraught with greater difficulties of social control. As this study demonstrates, the problems here created require insight, tolerance, and patience on the part of both peoples. Such volumes as this can help provide the insight which is a *sine qua non* of both tolerance and patience.

HOWARD E. JENSEN

Durham, N. C.
August 10, 1953

PREFACE

The various Spanish-speaking groups in the United States have been the subjects of literary treatment for over a hundred years. They are represented in poems, dramas, songs, novels, light nonfiction, reference works, textbooks, and a multitude of articles of popular or scholarly nature. As a rule, the descriptive or analytical treatment of this subject has been by single group or subgroup: Mexicans in southern Texas, Spanish Americans in isolated villages, Filipinos in California, Puerto Ricans in New York, or Mexicans in Minnesota. Never, to the author's knowledge, have there been brought together under one cover the salient facts and problems of all the major Spanish-speaking groups in the United States. To do so is the purpose of this work.

This broader kind of treatment is more useful and more needed at present than it was in the past. Since World War II particularly, more people than ever before have been aware of and interested in the problems of minorities. This interest and awareness has fostered a desire to be well informed on the subject and a search for easily accessible means for becoming so. At present good books exist on every minority group discussed in this volume, but by no means all of them are readily available, not all of them are easily comprehensible, and in size and price many of them lie beyond the lay reader's interest and means. This volume at-

tempts to present compactly yet understandably the more significant aspects of the life and conditions of each of our Spanish-speaking groups, so that such information may be easily available to the
growing number of persons who desire it.

These groups may legitimately be considered in one volume
since they all share, in varying degrees, a background of Spanish
culture. Each group shows the imprint of this culture, again in
varying degrees, on its language, its etiquette, its family structure
and mores, its religion, and its attitudes and values. The variations may be great, as between Puerto Rican and Filipino, or little
as between Mexican and Hispano-American, but in each case there
is a significant center of common Spanish origins in these webs of
culture.

The groups covered are, in the author's opinion, the most
significant ones. Discussion of Spaniards, Argentines, Peruvians,
Hondurans, Chileans, and Latin Americans in general is conspicuous by its absence. This omission was intentional. Other
than those included in this volume, the Spanish-speaking peoples in
the United States are so few in number as to be statistically insignificant. More to the point, almost nowhere (the Cubans of
Florida and the Pueblo Indians of New Mexico excepted) have
they settled as a group or been recognized as a unit. Most South
and Central Americans in this country are here for study, for
business, or for travel, and make at most an infinitesimal impact
on our society. They are usually accepted or rejected on the basis
of their own personal qualities, and neither look upon themselves
nor are treated as a minority. Since it is unlikely that this situation
will change in the foreseeable future, the author has excluded
these groups from this volume—with personal apologies to any
Latin Americans who may feel slighted as a result.

JOHN H. BURMA

Grinnell College
Grinnell, Iowa

CONTENTS

LIST OF MAPS

Spanish-Speaking Groups
in the United States

I.

DESCENDANTS OF SPANISH COLONIALS: THE HISPANOS OF NEW MEXICO

More than three hundred years ago the first Spaniards came to the northwestern outpost of Spain's empire, New Mexico. Mostly males, these soldiers and colonists married women of the indigenous Indian population. The resulting generations spoke Spanish, but developed a culture which was a mixture of the Spanish and Indian and which, before long, took on a flavor all its own. Numerous agricultural and stock-raising communities were established, mostly on land grants from the Spanish crown. The typical community had a plaza, four streets running outward, houses close in, small agricultural plots and orchards near by, and beyond in a great circle the *edijo*, common land, used for grazing stock, recreation, and obtaining building materials. Theirs was not commercial but subsistence farming and stock raising. Since that time the descendants of these colonists have lived on the same land, spoken the same tongue, and retained in remarkable degree the culture of eighteenth-century Spain.

Historical Background. These communities automatically became a part of Mexico after the Mexican Revolution, and were annexed to the United States after the Mexican War in 1846. Throughout these changes the New Mexicans maintained their isolation; New Mexico was their homeland and the object of their first loyalty. New Mexico is, in many respects, an extension of Latin America into United States territory. Linguistically and culturally New Mexico has as many ties with South as with North America.[1] These descendants of the Spanish colonists prefer not to be called "Mexicans"; they prefer the terms "Spanish American" or "Hispano." Before annexation, people from the United States were called "Americanos." After annexation, since both were "Americanos," the terms "Hispano-Americano" and "Anglo-Americano" were used and were soon shortened to "Hispano" and "Anglo." Hispanos reserve the term "Mexican" for residents of or immigrants from Mexico. This same class pattern of old settlers and newcomers is to be found in southern California and in Colorado, where both Hispanos and Anglos feel that they rank above the recently immigrated Mexicans. In the northern Colorado beet area, for example, there is little co-operation or even social contact between these two Spanish-speaking groups, and in some towns they live in separate slums, looking down on each other.

Little intermarriage has taken place between the Hispanos and Mexicans, less between the Hispanos and Anglos, and in the last hundred years surprisingly little between the Hispanos and the Indians. Since the early period of miscegenation, the Hispano and the Indian have generally held aloof from each other, although there are some cases of more tolerant Indian pueblos' disintegrating

---

[1] John H. Burma, "The Present Status of Spanish Americans in New Mexico," *Social Forces*, XXVIII (Dec., 1949), 133-38.

as Indian city-states and becoming mixed Spanish villages.[2] Hispanos, like the Indians, suffered by becoming a part of the United States and its radically different economic structure. They, like the Indians, needed to be educated deliberately into actual as well as nominal American citizenship and to be protected economically and socially while this education was going on. Because no such steps were taken, Spanish Americans have more than an equitable share of economic and social problems.

Populational Aspects. Spanish Americans form a higher proportion of the population of New Mexico than does any other minority group in any other state. Estimates of the population whose mother tongue is Spanish range from 44.5 per cent to 53.3 per cent plus those upper-class, urban Spanish Americans whose mother tongue (the language spoken in the home) is English. Because of the equality in numbers, it is not so surprising that both English and Spanish are official languages; voting instructions are in both languages, a suspect may plead before the court in Spanish, and only recently was it made mandatory that schools be conducted in English. The 1940 census reports 192,820 persons in New Mexico whose mother tongue is Spanish and who were born to native parents. Almost all of this group are Hispanos. According to Carey McWilliams[3] Hispanos comprise 50 per cent or more of the population in each of 15 out of 31 counties, and these 15 counties have almost 60 per cent of the population of the state. In each of seven counties, Spanish-speaking people constitute more than 80 per cent of the population. The map facing page 7 indicates the location of the Spanish Americans in New Mexico. A scattering of these descendants of the Spanish colonials live in

[2] Cf. Ruth Laughlin, "Coronado's Country and Its People," *Survey Graphic*, XXIX (May, 1940), 277-82.

[3] Carey McWilliams, *Brothers Under the Skin* (Boston: Little, Brown and Company, 1943), p. 128.

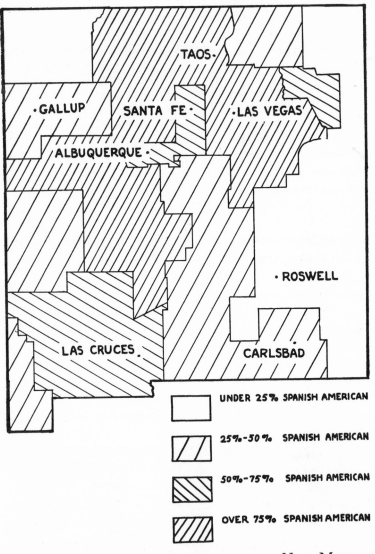

DISTRIBUTION OF SPANISH AMERICANS IN NEW MEXICO

Colorado, Texas, Arizona, and California, but nowhere except in New Mexico are they a truly significant populational element.

Community. It is impossible to overemphasize the importance of the home village to the Spanish American. Most Hispanos would be better off financially elsewhere, and they know it. Yet they either remain in or return to the village as filings cling and return to a magnet. Young adults desire and expect to return to their village; this is one of the reasons the older people retain their village holdings so tenaciously. The father feels obligated to bequeath his land to his sons and daughters. As a minority group with its own language and with strong customs and traditions, the Hispanos are ill at ease with the Anglos, who look down on them and whose antipathy drives them more closely into their own group for appreciation and self-expression. Only at home in their own community can they relax and feel at ease.

The physical structure of the Hispano community is also a significant factor in its integration and stability.[4] The houses are compactly located with the barns and corrals in the rear and school, church, and store in the center. Houses are one-story adobe, and are replastered yearly. Extremely picturesque and unspoiled by tourists, these villages are none the less rural slums of the first order. Electricity, telephones, window screens, and an indoor water supply are rare or nonexistent. This Old World village pattern is rather inefficient from the agricultural viewpoint, but it makes possible the development and integration of group life and institutions not possible under any other system.[5] Childhood associations are almost as

[4] Cf. Olen Leonard and C. P. Loomis, *Culture of a Contemporary Rural Community: El Cerrito, New Mexico* (Rural Life Studies, No. 1 [Washington: U. S. Department of Agriculture, 1941]), pp. 7-8. Hereinafter referred to as *El Cerrito*.

[5] For an excellent discussion of the merits of various types of rural communities, see T. Lynn Smith, *The Sociology of Rural Life* (New York: Harper and Brothers, 1947), chaps. x-xi.

close between playmates as between siblings. Marriage within the village is common, so that each village is made up of a few large kinship groups. New Mexico law, and more importantly the church, forbids marriage between second cousins, so that most marital relationships within the recognized kinship group are those of third cr fourth cousin. Such relationships are insignificant in modern urban society, but are kept close track of in the isolated Hispano villages and are considered real ties of blood. The net result is that the sense of community is strong in most Spanish Americans. Individuals are still identified by the community of which they are members, and loyalty to the community and its people reaches a degree unknown in most of the United States.

Family. The colonists of New Spain brought with them a highly integrated pattern of social life, built around the family and the church. Each of these institutions aided and supported the other; both were authoritarian. The authority of the father was unquestioned and the oldest male was a patriarch whose authority was widely felt. He could fix the group opinion about any current problem or event. He made decisions about the crops, the work, and the share allotted each individual. If the head of a family group lived to a ripe old age, his sons and grandsons frequently worked in a community of ownership under the direction of the head of the hierarchy. Often such a group of families lived in adjoining houses in a distinct section of the village.

The role of the woman has always been a subordinate one in Spanish cultures, but it has been extremely important in the stability and integration of the group. A woman is expected to be faithful to the church even though her husband, like so many Anglo husbands, "has his religion in his wife's name." Her interests, both in theory and in practice, are in producing children and caring for her family and her home. She is not encouraged to move outside this sphere, and she rarely steps far outside her prescribed role, for in a small community the primary social controls operate effectively. Ostracism, even partial, is no light blow when visiting and conversation with other women offer the only release from the drab drudgery of housework and child care in a poverty-stricken home.

The role of the man is less restricted. He is expected to assume material responsibility for his wife and children, to be loyal to the large family group, and to live up to his community responsibilities. His private morals are pretty much his own business, but his social morals must be above reproach if he is to have any status in the community. He may, for example, get drunk occasionally without being reprimanded, but stealing or niggardliness are unforgivable offenses.[6]

⟨Dominant Values and Attitudes. The old living pattern of the early colonists still persists in many ways. At no point is it more apparent than in the practice of cooperation and mutual aid.[7] Strongest between related families, this pattern is still community-wide and efforts are still pooled in any endeavor that necessitates it. Tools and equipment are privately owned but are loaned and borrowed very freely. Uncritical and superficial observers have spoken of the Spanish Americans' completely common ownership of equipment; it does not exist. It is true, however, that long propinquity to close kin and the same neighbors has fused with the heritage of communal land-ownership to create an attitude toward private ownership of property which is often totally unlike that of the Anglos.

⟨Among the American traditions handed down by our Puritan ancestors is that thrift and hard work are virtues in themselves. No such values exist among the Spanish

---

[6] Leonard and Loomis, El Cerrito, pp. 15-19.
[7] Much of the material here presented on attitudes and values is drawn from Leonard and Loomis, El Cerrito, pp. 15-63.

Americans. Idleness and leisure are not sinful corruption but worthwhile goals to be sought. Hard work is the common and accepted lot, but it is a necessity, a means to an end, not a virtue. Children go to work early and age brings no surcease, but the value of work lies in what it brings in the way of possessions, land, and independence. Work is likely to be carried on at moderate tempo. Where manpower is greater than available work, haste would result in excessive idleness. The Hispano prefers to work moderately rather than sporadically; he stops to chat with friends, to take a siesta, and then proceeds with his work at a rather leisurely pace. Although they work long and hard under seasonal pressures, Hispanos seem to lack interest in steady daily output. Having such habit patterns they are bored with the infinite repetitions of a factory. Conversely, at handcraft they excel, but there is little place for handcraft in our modern machine technology.

Spanish Americans are a neighborly people. Through years of interdependence, they are conditioned to call upon neighbors and relatives for many types of assistance and, in turn, are expected to reciprocate when the need arises. In case of sickness or similar misfortune, the efforts and resources of the entire village may be utilized in order to bring the family through the crisis. This neighborliness is particularly noticeable in the custom of visiting between families. Such visiting is the chief mode of contact between villagers, and children are continually running in and out of each others' homes. The visiting of women exceeds that of men; the degree of blood relationship seems to be the chief factor affecting the frequency of these visits.[8] The individual's loyalties and responsibilities are closely tied to the local village group. During the child's formative years he seldom sees the outside world, and he soon becomes accustomed to identifying himself with his village.

[8] Charles P. Loomis, "Informal Groupings in a Spanish-American Village," *Sociometry*, IV (Feb., 1941), 40-51.

For many adults the outside world is strange and foreign
and beyond comprehension. The Hispano is truly at ease
only in his home village.

The Hispano man is expected to support his immediate
family and to aid his parents and near relatives when they
are in need. Otherwise he is allowed wide freedom of
action. It is the wife who has the responsibility of setting
the example for the family. The girl is taught early that
her place is in the home. She must be pure, religious, and
obedient to her husband. Her complete life is devoted to
her home and family, and dealings with the outside world
are left to the husband.

During the disturbing crises in national and world affairs since 1941, there has been an observable decline in
family and community control. Tradition and custom play
a lesser role both quantitatively and qualitatively. The
father is more likely to be only the titular head of his
family or of the families of married sons. This does not
indicate real friction, for family love and respect are strong
and deep-rooted. It does indicate an awareness on the
part of young men, especially veterans, that they know
many things, can do many things, and can judge many
things which their fathers cannot. There is somewhat
less change in the role of women, for they have not so
readily found employment outside the village. Young
wives have more voice in family affairs than their mothers
did, and the authority of the wife's mother-in-law has
observably declined, even though overt friction is rare.
Even in the younger families the husband is still the head
of the house, and he goes his own way—to town without
taking his wife, for example. Some of these changes stem
from an increasing preference of young men, especially
veterans, for Spanish-American girls from towns or cities.
The young men's commonest explanation is that these girls
are "better educated," which is probably true, and that

they are "more fun," which seems to mean that these town girls play a less proscribed female role than do the village girls. When such a bride moves to a village she is less likely to accept the old forms of authority and control, and if difficulties arise, she may persuade her husband to move to one of the larger towns near-by.[9]

There is less decline in family unity and authority among the beetworker minority; the whole family migrates, earnings are pooled, and the father is the economic as well as the social authority. This decline is somewhat counteracted by the fact that the beetworking group is least interested in community affairs and tends, even when present in the village, to be somewhat peripheral socially.

Leadership and Class. Historically the *dons* of each local village controlled the land, the stock, the jobs, and hence the villagers. Such a class structure existed in rural New Mexico for a century, but it has tended to disappear along with the economic situation on which it was based. In some villages there are families which still control a large part of the economic life of the village. Yet these families, often merchants, would incur ruinous ostracism if they carried class distinction to an extreme. As a rule, such families are descendants of the local *dons* or *patrons*, but they are likely to be interrelated by marriage with most of the families of the village.

Where such families exist they still exert some leadership. Other leaders, especially for local affairs, are those who combine within themselves the three qualities of age, family, and verbal fluency.[10] For nonlocal matters the rural Hispanos are increasingly turning to townsmen for advice and leadership. Townspeople are better informed, and in the increasingly modernized world of the Hispanos experience and prestige no longer outweigh information

[9] Frank E. Wilson, "El Cerrito—A Changing Culture" (Master's thesis, New Mexico Highlands University, 1949).

[10] *Ibid.*, pp. 58-59.

and knowledge as guides for individual and community life.

Economic Aspects. The economic foundation of the Hispanos always has been a combination of stock raising and subsistence agriculture. The early settlers owned reasonably large irrigated farms and either owned or freely used vast acreages of grazing land on the surrounding mesas. On their irrigated land they grew more than enough food for themselves and their livestock, and on the mesa they grazed the herds of sheep and cattle which represented their chief form of wealth.

The ultimate source of all wealth in the mountains of New Mexico is water—a scarce commodity. Springs are few, but constantly flowing streams run down from the snow-covered peaks of the Sierras. Wherever these pass through arable land, that land is likely to be made productive by irrigation. Dry farming is almost an impossibility in most of New Mexico. Unfortunately the amount of arable land and water is strictly limited. Functioning on its stable land base, a community in Spanish times may have been prosperous and relatively self-sufficient economically. The land base today is about the same, but the population is not. On land that once supported 10 families in comfort, 100 families may live now in poverty. Although New Mexico has a population density of only 4 persons per square mile, some of the irrigated areas of the Rio Grande Valley have a population of well over 500 persons per square mile, making these some of the most densely populated rural areas in the whole United States.

The system of dividing land equally among all the heirs is equitable, but in the case of the Hispanos it has been disastrous. Such is the community and family integration of the Spanish American that he has been extremely loath to leave his home village. As a result population has increased, size of holdings has decreased, and today some so-called "farms" are no more than 20 yards wide and 100 yards long. It is no wonder that 90 per cent of the rural families get less than substistence from farming; 80 per cent of these farms have less than 15 acres and the average is about 10 acres, of which only 6 to 8 are actually cultivated. In some areas fragmentation has reduced irrigated land to as little as ⅒ to ⅛ of an acre, and mesa land to 80 to 160 acres (40 to 50 acres are needed for one cow-unit). In such an agricultural situation tractors are uncommon and are a symbol of financial success. Some trend toward concentration of landownership is found, with land usually going to families which have some members working outside the community, to veterans, or to others with access to cash. A family cannot wrest a proper level of living from such a base even if the land is exceptionally good, which this land is not. Corn, alfalfa, red chilis, and garden produce are grown on the irrigated land, wheat, corn, and beans on the dry farming land. The corn is the native flint or Indian blue corn, so hard it must be ground even before being fed to livestock. County agents are trying, without outstanding success, to introduce modern corn. Cattle are the major cash crop, with sheep and goats declining because they are hard on the land and require a herder. Pigs and chickens are raised for food.[11] The irrigated land produces the crops which the Hispano must have. He plants his dry land in whatever else he wishes. If he raises a crop, he eats more, feeds his stock better, and has a little to sell. If drought occurs, as it frequently does, he tightens his belt and his stock becomes gaunt. Food is usually adequate during the garden season, and there is some attempt to preserve produce for winter food.

But what of the hundreds of thousands of acres of mesa grazing land which once supported huge herds of sheep

[11] *Ibid.*

and cattle? Under the laws adopted after the Mexican War, the United States theoretically recognized the claim of the inhabitants to all the land rights proved by Spanish grant. Unfortunately, these grants were vague, not accurately recorded, and subject to expensive litigation. Much of the grazing land used by the Hispanos before American occupation had been tacitly recognized as belonging to the community it surrounded. Actually it was part of the early public domain and was taken over by the state. In all, less than half the land once owned or used by the Hispanos was ever confirmed in title to a Spanish American. That which did remain in Hispano hands has been subject to the same ruinous subdivision as has irrigated land. Moreover, grazing land on the mesas is poor. A pasture for a single herd of sheep must be measured in hundreds of acres. Anglo ranches characteristically are measured by square miles. A person accustomed to thinking in terms of Midwestern or Southern farms of 80 to 160 acres finds it difficult to realize that a square mile of land may rent for less than $50.00 a year, or even go begging with no one willing to rent or buy it at any price.

As if this ruinous subdivision were not enough of a problem, New Mexico like most states has a real property tax which makes possible foreclosure for nonpayment of taxes. For the past 25 years, more and more Spanish-American land has been sold, a portion at a time, to pay delinquent taxes on the remainder. Regardless of its justice, the net effect of the land tax has been to transfer much land from the small and rather inefficiently managed farms and ranches of the Spanish Americans to the larger and more efficiently operated holdings of the Anglos. Since 1854 Hispanos have lost 2,000,000 acres of private land, 1,700,000 acres of communal land, 1,800,000 acres have been taken by the state for its educational fund, and vast areas have been given to railroads or placed in national forests.

In short, these hereditary agriculturists and stock raisers have access to an insufficient land base to support themselves and their families. If they had more land they could continue their generations-old way of life. As it is, wagework, preferably near at home and probably for an Anglo, is about the only independent solution to the problem. The Hispanos want land, they buy it when they can, but it is rarely possible for them to amass sufficient cash for such a purpose. Improved use of the land is, of course, a possibility. In many ways Hispano practices today are on a par with those of a century ago. The visitor may see irrigation dams made of mud, stones, and brush, irrigation conduits made of hand-hollowed half-logs, hand-hewn flumes, and shallow hand-dug irrigation ditches. Farm machinery is simple and old-fashioned. Grain is still often harvested with a scythe and threshed by the hooves of horses, goats, or cattle. Yet improved agricultural practices are not the solution. A family with five acres may double its productivity and still be far from self-supporting. Such programs are of value only to those farmers who are marginal, who barely fail to make a living. Teaching improved techniques to those who are very submarginal may actually be a disservice, tying them still more tightly to an inevitably insufficient land base. The Hispano-American is likely to feel that timesaving and laborsaving devices are of minor importance. They mean little when manpower is already in excess of the work to be done.

The oldest and most important economic association in any village is likely to be one whose purpose is to clean, repair, control, and maintain the irrigation system. There are no fees and no profits. Each family using the irrigation water is included and must contribute labor in accordance with the area of land operated. A "ditch boss" is elected. His function is to inspect the main ditch, supervise its cleaning, and call out the men whenever repairs are needed. An elected committee distributes the water according to need and supply.

The Spanish American, in general, is not susceptible to modification of his farming attitudes and practices. He must depend to a considerable or preponderant extent on outside labor, and full-time farming is dying out more and more. The Hispano loves his land, and nearly all Hispanos own a little land or expect to inherit some, but it has come to mean a home and a large garden, not a farm. The Hispano is a stockman by preference, not a farmer. He farms because he has to grow things to eat, not because he prefers agriculture as a way of life. Today he is a stockman almost without stock. Each family has a horse, possibly several, some have a milch cow or a hog, most families have a few chickens. The scarceness of livestock arises largely from a lack of available pasture reasonably close to the village. What livestock the Hispanos do have is likely to be of a scrubby, hardy breed, usually poor and carelessly tended. Better livestock could hardly be cared for properly even if it were available.

The typical Hispano farmer owns and operates ten irrigated acres. He has a team, a milch cow or two, three, or four beef cattle, a dozen chickens, and possibly a couple of hogs. His farm equipment is simple, often borrowed or owned in common with neighbors or kinsmen. The five- or six-person family lives in a four-room adobe house furnished with cheap furniture, partly handmade. They grow a little wheat for flour, alfalfa, corn, beans, chilis, and some garden vegetables. The net yield is about $20.00 per acre. This is obviously too meager; so the father or grown son works on a sheep camp, on a ranch,

in the beet fields, or worked on WPA projects when they
were available.[12]

⟨ For a generation before the 1930's the Hispano way
of life necessarily included work away from home. Hired
labor had always been common, but it permitted the
worker to live at home most of the time. Gradually this
locus was expanded and Hispano males went farther and
farther afield as migratory workers. This disturbed family
and community patterns but little, for the migrant was
always assumed to be away temporarily and his home remained in the village. With the onset of the depression
this source of income practically ceased, and serious poverty resulted. The Federal Emergency Relief Program
was the only straw at which these people could grasp and
they did so with the tenacity of drowning men. Stock
raising and agriculture were replaced by wage labor, and
wage labor was replaced by government subsidy as the
chief source of income. Not all of the various assistance
programs were received with equal warmth, however.
The WPA was by all odds the most popular and useful.
The people wanted to work and they needed money desperately. They were interested in the Farm Security
Administration program but refused to participate because it necessitated a mortgage on their remaining tiny
holdings. The villages are typically overpopulated; so
the CCC camps and NYA were doubly beneficial. It is
impossible to overemphasize the value of government
relief programs to the Hispano villagers. Without such
programs their traditional way of life would have disappeared and they along with it.

During the depression the New Mexico State Department of Vocational Education began work among the Hispanos. When the war boom occurred, they increased their

[12] Allen G. Harper, Andrew R. Cordova, and Kaleroo Oberg, *Man and
Resources in the Middle Rio Grande Valley* (Albuquerque, N. M.: University of New Mexico Press, 1943), pp. 70-72.

program of teaching industrial skills and placed hundreds of Spanish-American trainees in war industries. Here most of them made good wages for the first time; and at types of manufacturing which required hand skill and co-ordination of hand and eye the Hispanos made a particularly good record.

Education. New Mexico ranks sixth among the states in amount of illiteracy; over a quarter of the population has had four years or less of schooling and one-tenth have had no schooling at all. The Hispanos are largely responsible for this poor record. As is true of all marginal groups, the public school is a major factor in introducing American culture patterns to the Hispanos. Young and old realize that the English language is essential to success, and the school is the chief means of acquiring that language. The New Mexico law now requires that only English be spoken in the schools. Hispano teachers and pupils are likely to adhere to the spirit rather than to the letter of the law. A first-grade class with no English-speaking members obviously must use Spanish as a medium. Even in much later grades the student, or even the teacher, will use a Spanish word or phrase if the English one does not come readily to mind.[13] Poor attendance, mediocre teaching, and early withdrawal from school prevent the acquisition of much proficiency. Progress in any subject tends to be below average. Relating the pupils' needs to the subject matter is even less usual than in non-Hispano schools. During the school year 1939-40, the pupils of El Cerrito worked out posters and other projects

[13] This habit is by no means to be condemned. It does indicate failure to reach the standard prescribed, but there is increasing evidence that bilingual instruction, particularly as an initial instrument, may be more efficient educationally, even in teaching English. The present system is somewhat analogous to throwing a child into the water to teach him to swim: he may learn to stay afloat, but he will not become a finished swimmer. Experiments are also under way in which the child is first taught vocal English, then written Spanish, and then written English.

based on such subjects as transportation in Boston and the importance of navigation in the growth of Chicago. Under such a curriculum as this it is no small wonder that pupil interest is at a minimum and progress is slow.

According to Albuquerque teachers, "lack of speaking knowledge of English on entering school" and "failure to read English with comprehension" were the two most important factors in the retardation of Mexican children.[14] A state survey of reading in the elementary schools of New Mexico showed Spanish-speaking students considerably below the standard in both comprehension and rate.[15] Educational mortality of Hispano youth is high. According to Dr. Sanchez's study, of the 60,000 Spanish-speaking children enrolled in school, over one-third were in the first grade and over one-half were in the first three grades. Fifty-five per cent of those above the first grade were more than two years overage for their grades.[16] Most Hispano children attend rural schools, and to their special difficulties are added the nationwide rural problems of inadequate teachers and inadequate financial support. Students from rural areas can rarely do high-school work in a larger town, even when they have the opportunity. In general, the more highly urbanized the child's community, the more likely he is to go to high school and to pass his work. In the towns there is also a considerable amount of parochial schooling, ranging from poor to excellent in quality, which serves as a supplement. Basic to the whole problem is the fact that, in general, the higher the percentage of Spanish-speaking people in a county, the lower the per capita assessed valuation and the poorer the schools. In

[14] M. C. Taylor, "Retardation of Mexican Children in Albuquerque Schools" (Master's thesis, Stanford University, Palto Alto, California, 1927).

[15] Harlan Sininger, "New Mexico's Reading Survey" (Master's thesis, University of New Mexico, Albuquerque, New Mexico, 1930).

[16] G. I. Sanchez, *Forgotten People* (Albuquerque, N. M.: University of New Mexico Press, 1940), pp. 30-31.

such counties, school terms are shorter, teachers are less well prepared and are paid lower salaries, and school buildings and instruction materials are inferior to those found in other parts of New Mexico.

One of the brighter spots in the Spanish Americans' educational possibilities is New Mexico's vocational education program, which has been made possible by federal funds since 1921. It serves youth of high-school age who cannot go to college and ex-high-school students who are now wage earners. Although the program is for both Anglo and Hispano, extensive experiments were made before the war in semi-isolated Spanish-American villages where people turned to crafts to supplement their low agricultural incomes. Emphasis was on blacksmithing, carpentry and woodworking, tanning and leatherwork, ironwork, weaving, and the making of rustic furniture. With the coming of World War II, emphasis changed to metalworking for industrial war work, including aircraft-engine work, riveting, welding, and auto mechanics. Since the end of the war the program has been extended to include skills such as merchandising, fire service, meat-cutting, oil-field training, electricity, and cosmetology. Valuable though this program is, the number of Spanish Americans who can attend college is very small, and the number cannot nearly reach its potential maximum because of the inadequate previous training provided most of the potential students. Only with the coming of veterans' educational benefits has any appreciable number of Spanish Americans been able to attend college.

Health. The health situation of the Hispanos is as bad as one would expect in a poverty-stricken, culturally backward group.[17] The 1921-38 death rate per 1,000 in the United States was 10.3 for whites, with a low of 7.7

[17] The following material is drawn largely from Harper *et al., Man and Resources,* pp. 109-12.

for North Dakota and a high of 16.2 for New Mexico. In New Mexico the group of counties with the highest death rates is the same group of counties that has the highest percentage of Spanish Americans. When the national infant mortality rate was 78.4 per 1,000 live births, it was 108.6 in Taos County, 118.9 in Rio Arriba, 131.4 in Socorro, 135.0 in Valencia, and 168.6 in Sandoval County. Maternal mortality in New Mexico is about half again as great as the national average. The lack of prenatal care, the fact that in many Hispano villages 85 per cent to 90 per cent of the births are handled by midwives, and the nutritionally defective diet commonly given infants help account for the fact that only about 60 per cent of Hispano children reach adulthood. In some counties from one-half to three-quarters of all deaths are registered as from unknown causes. This indicates that few such deaths were attended by competent physicians. New Mexico is nationally famous as a place of rest and cure for tuberculous patients, yet the tuberculosis rates of New Mexico are the highest in the nation. In some predominantly Hispano counties the rate is as high as one in every two children of school age. As the result of a diet too high in carbohydrates and too low in vitamins, rickets and other constitutional diseases are often very prevalent, striking as high as four out of five children in some villages. In Taos County, with a population over 90 per cent Spanish-American, the most common diseases were infections of the upper respiratory or the pulmonary system, dental infection, infectious diseases of childhood, and genitourinary infections.

A study of causes of death was made for six sample counties, three with a high percentage of Spanish-American population, and three with a high percentage of Anglo-American population; the total population of each group was the same. Striking differences may be observed in the table below.[18]

[18] Adapted from tables in "Vital Statistics in New Mexico," *New Mexico Health Officer*, X (July, 1942), 4-5.

NUMBER AND CAUSES OF DEATHS

Cause	Spanish-American counties	Anglo-American counties
Tuberculosis.............	126	34
Pneumonia..............	95	39
Diarrhea and enteritis...	89	12
Puerperal sepsis, etc......	25	5
Venereal disease.........	33	6
Homicide..............	6	7
Ill-defined and unknown causes..............	656	43

A study was also made of the New Mexico counties which ranked in the upper half in infant mortality. In this upper half were found all 8 of the counties with the highest percentage of Spanish-American population and only 2 of the 8 with the highest percentage of Anglo population. The 8 counties with the highest percentage of Spanish-American population had one medical doctor for every 2,867 persons, and one hospital for every 17,563 persons. The 8 counties with the highest percentage of Anglo population had one medical doctor for every 2,286 persons and one hospital for every 11,610 persons.[19]

One need not be a competent medical authority to recognize important causal factors in (1) poverty, (2) inadequate diet, (3) ignorance of personal hygiene and even of the germ theory of disease, (4) reliance on home remedies or herb doctors, (5) ministrations of incompetent and even amateur midwives, and (6) primitive sanitation and consequent water pollution. The most hopeful fact is that most of these difficulties are not insurmountable. An efficient, widespread rural health program with special emphasis on prevention and hygiene education, on sanitation, and on diet, plus the means of putting this knowledge into

[19] Data from various recent, undated, mimeographed releases by the New Mexico Department of Public Health.

effect, could in one generation make the basically sound Hispano stock one of the healthiest in the nation.

Religion. For the Spanish colonists the church was one of the most powerful institutions. Its domination arosé not alone from religious authority but also from its initiation of such forms of social participation as fiestas, games, and dances. Even the activities of daily life, conduct, and functions of the family were tremendously influenced by the authoritarian church, for the Hispanos are a devout people, almost 100 per cent Roman Catholic. Although little extra money is available, a way is found to burn the necessary candles and to acquire a new costume for a child's first Communion. The church is likely to be the best-kept building in the village. The women are especially devout, and they rigidly observe holy days. The training of children in the knowledge and practices of the Church is begun at an early age.

The priest is recognized not only as a spiritual leader, but as a source of temporal advice and community leadership. Because villages are usually so small, a parish may include from five to ten villages. Although the priest may come only once a month, services are held every week or even more often, with a local woman in charge. The services are well attended and the hymns and ritual are well learned, even by the illiterate. No doubt the period of general conversation after the service has something to do with the excellence of the attendance. Most major, and some minor, Protestant denominations maintain mission churches here and there among the Hispanos, but the number of converts probably does not reach 5 per cent.

Although the higher church officials disapprove, one of the most bizarre aspects of Spanish-American religion, the sect of Los Hermanos de los Penitentes, remains a powerful force (see Appendix I). Some of the beliefs of the penitential and flagellant societies, which arose in southern Europe in the fourteenth and fifteenth centuries, were brought to New Mexico by the early settlers and transmitted by them. Under the missionary friars there grew up a powerful lay Third Order of St. Francis: but when those friars were expelled a century and a quarter ago, the order took on strange, localized, and unauthorized forms. Although its liturgy and songs came direct from the medieval church, it became more and more a primitive penance and a primitive worship of death. The initiations and other rites became bloody, with members beating themselves with leather thongs, cactus whips, or even barbed wire. On Good Friday occurred a bloody penitential march to a hill where the crucifixion was dramatized so realistically that the *Cristo* sometimes died. Frowned upon by both church and state, adherents of the sect drew together into societies which became more and more secret.

The widest extension of these lurid practices occurred between 1850 and 1880, and even the outlawing of the sect by the bishop of that time did not cause it to die. Since the 1880's gradual changes have appeared; the number of adherents has declined, the geographic territory has shrunk, and the savagery of their self-torture has been much mitigated. Yet even now, in the isolated villages, there exist a *morada*, the meeting hall, a *Hermano major*, the leader, and, back in the hills, dozens of large crosses— some obviously recent. As Good Friday approaches, strange preparations still take place and strange rituals occur, and here and there blood still flows on the penitential march to the hill where the living Christ is still tied to the cross. No tourist attraction, much of the ceremony is secret, and stray visitors are gruffly warned that they trespass. But Easter is not the only period of activity for the Penitentes. Each local group has more or less regular meetings, and has a special ceremony on the day of its patron saint. In some cases these ceremonies also involve the self-infliction of pain. Whenever a member dies, a wake is held by all the members and their womenfolk. The women prepare food to be eaten at midnight. Before and after the meal the men sing *Alabaos*, the ritual mourning chants.

In each community the rules, attitudes, and behavior of the Penitentes differ. These customs have largely been orally transmitted, and over a period of many generations the isolated local cells have taken on considerable variation. Sometimes the *morada* is hidden far back in the mountains, sometimes it is inside the village itself. Some cells still have bloody crucifixion rituals; in others, blood has not flowed for two generations. Some initiation ceremonies include ritual scarification; some do not. Some cells permit relatively full participation of women; others exclude them almost completely. Some permit sympathetic outsiders to enter the *morada* for Lenten services; some do not. Some use many modern hymns; others cling almost entirely to sixteenth-century Spanish chants. Some individuals undoubtedly achieve a sort of spiritual rebirth and cleansing of great value; but one judge reports sentencing a *Cristo* for horse theft before his scars had completely healed.

Strongest in the predominantly Spanish-American north central area, in the Sangre de Cristo Mountains the order has taken on strong political aspects. With its increase in political power and its decline in savagery has come formal recognition from the Catholic church, given by the archbishop of Santa Fe in 1946. According to one historian, the present penitential order "has so degenerated that it is nothing today but an anomalous body of simple, credulous men, under the guidance of some unscrupulous politicians."[20]

[20] R. E. Twitchell, *Leading Facts of New Mexico History* (Cedar Rapids, Iowa: The Torch Press, 1912), II, 168.

Recreation. For obvious reasons, recreation among the Hispanos is likely to be limited to forms in which one may indulge for little or no cash. Dances are the most common formal type; "going to town" (for villagers, the nearest town or city; for urban dwellers, the business district) and conversational visiting are the most important informal types. Political rallies, weddings, and feast days occasionally add their bit. In most communities a weekly dance is held. A small admission charge pays for the permit required in New Mexico; any extra goes to the local-talent orchestra which will usually play without any set compensation. Young and old attend. The young people dance; the older persons watch, gossip, talk politics and exchange news. The boys and girls do not come together, leave together, or sit together when not dancing. The old dances—*raspa*, polka, and quadrille—are not forgotten, though modern dancing is better liked.[21]

Politics. Hispanos have always been interested in their government, but in a narrow and self-centered fashion. This pattern was augmented by their relationships with governmental welfare activities. A candidate for any office is appraised in terms of "what can he do for us?" His attitude toward basic issues is passed over lightly; he is measured in terms of possible jobs, grants, or relief. Most candidates, nevertheless, make use of the time-honored methods of impressing constituents, free dances, and free drinks. Some political clubs exist, particularly among the younger villagers. Politics being what it is, there usually are two clubs in a village or at least two factions within the one club. The feeling arose during the depression that one must be friendly with the *politicos*, that a person will benefit from government programs in proportion to his participation in politics and his strong political friends. Unfortunately, many Hispano and non-

[21] Leonard and Loomis, *El Cerrito*, pp. 49-50.

Hispano politicians continue to foster this attitude for their own purposes. Although Hispanos hold the balance of political power in New Mexico, their cultural inadequacy causes them to be "political stepchildren," as if they were a small minority. Here and there a Hispano achieves political importance. Senators Chavez and Larrazola are examples—but the practical political strength of the Hispano is so slight that he has not even been able to block what little discriminatory legislation New Mexico has, and only by complete unanimity of the Spanish-American state legislators was New Mexico's weak Fair Employment Practices Act passed. The retention of both English and Spanish as official languages is probably their greatest political achievement.

Isolation and Discrimination. The people of the Spanish villages in New Mexico have limited means of contact with the outside world. There is no clearer commentary on their isolation than the fact that a number of Hispano villages do not have even one filling station. There is a low degree of dependence even between neighboring villages. Roads are extremely poor, often impassable during inclement weather. Automobiles and trucks are rather rare and are likely to serve as hired transportation for many others than their owners. This means that some transportation is occasionally available to any villager, but the occasions on which it is actually used are not frequent. As a consequence, local geography is imperfectly understood. In traveling between villages the author often spoke with youngsters of high-school age who did not know accurately the distance to near-by towns or villages, and who did not even know which roads led toward which towns. This was not a language handicap, for when the conversations were in Spanish the youngsters were at just as much of a loss, only more volubly so. Few newspapers come regularly to the Hispano villages, and few magazines except those of a religious nature appear. All are likely to be in Spanish. Radios, though not common, probably in the future will form the most important type of communication.

Except for those families who moved to town to secure WPA assistance, no considerable migration has ever occurred. Younger people form the bulk of migrants, and the older people offer few objections to such a movement, since it relieves the pressure of population in the home village. The rural-urban change is not an extreme one. Housing, household conveniences, and general culture are not very different in the section of the city into which the Hispano typically moves. There is some feeling of difference and sophistication on the part of the townsman, but no enmity or ill-will.

Outside his home village, and particularly in the larger cities, the Hispano meets some discrimination. It is of the type usually leveled at the Jew rather than at the Negro. This is to say, the Hispano in New Mexico may go to any school, be served at any cafe, stay at any hotel, ride anywhere in the streetcars or get a haircut at any barbershop. He likely will not be accepted socially, will have difficulty in securing employment commensurate with his ability, and may lose his turn to an Anglo when standing in line. He will likely live in a considerably segregated area, will drink his beer in a predominantly Hispano-patronized bar, and will attend his own dances and social functions. These latter types of segregation are of course more passive than active, for the Hispano is likely to be both proud and polite, but they are segregation none the less and make him slightly less likely to attempt urban migration.

World War II. The Hispano displays much loyalty to his family group and to his local village, and he is far from lacking in allegiance to the United States. Like the Indian, he does not allow historic ill-use to interfere with present loyalty. Everyone remembers the heroic retreat to Bataan in World War II, but few people know that the Two Hundredth and Five Hundred and Fifteenth Coast Artillery, which covered that retreat, were from New Mexico. They were sent to the Philippines both because they had antiaircraft units and because they spoke Spanish. One-fourth of those lost on Bataan were from New Mexico, most of them Spanish Americans. There were no segregated units, and Spanish Americans later served in all theaters and all branches. In many villages the local draft board was largely a figurehead—each boy volunteered as soon as he was acceptable. Although most of these young men showed a regrettable lack of insight into the fundamental, international ramifications of the war effort, they were very patriotic in a provincial sense, and had faith in and loyalty to the promise inherent in our democratic institutions, for it matched well their own ideals.

The poverty in which many of the veterans were reared, and their family solidarity, resulted in a considerable amount of their pay being sent home, where some of it was used if necessary, but most of it saved—even in buried fruit jars—for the boy's return. This, with mustering-out pay, was usually spent for something tangible, sometimes land or a tractor or a pump, more commonly a car or truck. Most of the veterans returned to their home villages, but many of them did not stay. The village is still "home," but they prefer to live and work outside the village, returning for visits. This attitude, plus the influence of the large number of villagers who held war jobs outside, has helped to break down more rapidly the previous isolation of many villages. Now nearly every family has some access to a car or a truck, and access now means use. The veterans' children will never be the isolated group their grandparents were.

Future. "Their [Hispanos'] present status is a vicious

downward spiral of ignorance, apathy, poverty, squalor, antiquated agricultural methods, badly balanced diets, shrinking and impoverished fields, resentment against discrimination, lack of confidence rooted in a feeling of inferiority, and exploitation by their own political leaders."[22] The above undoubtedly represents the pessimistic point of view, yet no eighteenth-century way of life is compatible with the middle of the twentieth century. Among the Hispanos today there is observable a growing feeling of futility, a general sense of inability to cope in the old ways with circumstances as they exist. They know what they want: to live in their own villages, to have a standard of living that is decent, if not comfortable, which they have provided for themselves through agriculture and livestock. What they do not know is how to implement their desires to achieve their goals. They have resisted change for decades; their resources are now at such an ebb that many of them, particularly the younger people, are convinced that a radical change in their way of life, however unpleasant or repugnant, is a necessity.

No such changes will come easily. A web of relationships based on the larger family institution enmeshes each individual. The family group is still both a social and economic entity. The co-operative obligations and rewards of family living are well defined; family interaction is basic. The new culture pattern so obviously needed would necessarily involve individualization, and individualization does not thrive in such a co-operative familial atmosphere. The inducement of WPA work during the thirties brought many families to the larger, non-Hispano towns. This physical separation from the home village has abetted individualization and change more than any other single factor.

[22] F. J. Brown and Joseph S. Roucek, *One America* (New York: Prentice-Hall, 1945), p. 352.

How serious this cultural change will be is a moot
question. Some Americans will say that such cultural
islands are predestined to be swallowed up in our competitive economy, that assimilation is inevitable, and the
sooner the better. Such a view, though partially valid,
assumes that the larger culture is in every particular better
than the minority culture, a situation which seldom if ever
exists. In fact, the Hispano culture offers many of those
things in which our own culture is so deficient. For three
centuries Hispanos have withstood drought and flood,
tilled the land faithfully, and maintained their sense of
community solidarity. They have a staying power we can
ill afford to throw away. Their interacting efficient family
structure is far superior in stability to our own divorce-
ridden one. Their filial respect, love of home and family,
and fortitude in the face of adversity all fit the American
ideal. California and Texas, among other states, could
benefit largely from the racial and ethnic tolerance found
among Hispanos. If we really want the good will of our
neighbors to the south, New Mexico and its Spanish-speaking people might well be the best bridge possible. In a
day of almost cutthroat competition the Hispano village
represents a noncommunistic form of co-operation between
persons who live and work in a compact social group.
Here a real social consciousness, even if limited in scope,
shines out to the larger individualistic society. Nor is this
only theory; Senator Dennis Chavez of New Mexico, himself a Hispano, sponsored important national social legislation and has been known as a definite liberal.

Educated Hispanos and some Anglos are beginning to
make real efforts to assist the Hispanos to help themselves.
Co-operative medical clinics and credit associations to tide
small farmers and craftsmen over short periods of financial
stress should work in any group with such a well-devel-
oped community sense. Possibly the way has been shown
by the Harwood Foundation in its Taos County project,

an effort to bring the needs of the villages in a rural county
into touch with the public and private agencies that are in
a position to render practical and constructive aid in social
as well as economic matters—a co-operative program of
community-county planning and practical action. Specifically, its efforts have resulted in the setting up of a Soil
Conservation District in the eastern half of the county,
the rehabilitation of the ditch system for the community of
Cerro, a loan to residents of Costilla and Amalia to re-
purchase a tax-delinquent tract of land, and a resident
Farm Security Administration agent. It has helped set up
the Taos County Co-operative Health Association, including some 12,000 people who were previously almost without medical assistance. It has sponsored a library and
visual education program with 11 branch libraries and a
bookmobile. It has assisted in setting up rural electrifica-
tion plans, secured school hot lunches in 23 communities,
has sponsored a recreational program, made a complete
socioeconomic survey of the county, and participated in
many minor but useful projects.

An entirely different approach—that of adult education by radio—was begun by New Mexico Highlands University (in the heart of the Hispano country) in 1943. Its
goals were assimilation, better sanitation and health practices, better soil use and conservation, an understanding of
governmental agencies, and greater understanding and appreciation of the rights and responsibilities of citizenship.
Previous attempts at adult education had foundered on the
bars of language, isolation, and aloofness. The proposed
solution was special broadcasts pitched at the proper level
of understanding, given in the Spanish language, and
aimed especially at radio-listening centers. Scholarships
were offered to 20 teachers in isolated Spanish-American
villages to attend the Institute of the Air at the university.
These people studied such matters as the sociology of
minorities, nutrition, health, sanitation, soil conservation,

the functions of governmental agencies, and the techniques of conducting a listening center and the discussion which should follow broadcasts. Out of the workshop grew radio scripts on the problems discussed. Then teachers, on returning to their villages, were paid for conducting the listening centers and for reporting results. While not as conspicuous a success as the Harwood Project, this technique has already proved itself valuable as an additional means of reaching the desired goals.

The problem of the Hispanos is more largely economic than that of other minorities. They desperately need more irrigated land, yet the total of such land is actually decreasing due to silt and floods. Much major construction is necessary, 50 to 100 million dollars' worth, so that the size of family-owned farms may be raised to above the subsistence level. Grazing lands considerably in excess of their present holdings are also needed, with co-operative grazing programs to insure their best use. But the Hispano can secure none of these things for himself, nor can the state of New Mexico give them to him. Only a long-range federal program of really substantial proportions can help the Hispano become again a self-sustaining farmer and stockman. The Forest Service, Reclamation Service, Soil Conservation Service and county agents, the Farm Security Administration and the Indian Service are co-operating to bring back the range. Since the Hispanos' problem is more largely economic than that of other minorities, this approach offers hope. Already, as of 1952, a major change can be observed in the pattern of land-ownership, with consolidation into fewer hands, a greater general prosperity and consequent increase in standards of living and of health and education, and increased assimilation resulting from the decline of the cultural, social, and familial unity and self-sufficiency of the village. The Church alone seems relatively unchanged.

II.

THE MEXICAN AMERICAN:
AN IMMIGRANT AND A WORKER

Although over a hundred years have passed since the southwestern part of the United States legally belonged to Mexico, Spanish-speaking people of old and new stock make up the largest minority in that region. Most of the remaining direct descendants of the old Spanish-colonial stock are concentrated in New Mexico, and since they hold themselves somewhat aloof from the later immigrants, they have been treated separately in the preceding chapter. The other scattered descendants of this early stock are few in number and widely distributed throughout the Southwest. They are reasonably well integrated into the more recently arrived group and hence will be considered as part of the Mexican-American rather than Spanish-American group.[1]

[1] Despite the custom by which many persons lump all Spanish-speaking persons indiscriminately into the category of *Mexicans,* we shall more precisely refer to those of Spanish colonial derivation as *Spanish Americans* or as *Hispanos;* those of Mexican parentage but United States citizenship will be called *Mexican Americans;* and those of recent emigration and Mexican

History and Population. It is impossible to give a completely accurate statement as to the number of Mexicans and Mexican Americans who now reside in the United States. The Bureau of the Census classifies as "white" and makes no separate count of those who are of Mexican extraction. The nearest census figure is that for those with "Spanish mother tongue," meaning those who habitually speak Spanish in the home, of whom there were 1,861,400 in 1940.[2] Of these, 428,360 were foreign-born, 714,060 were native white of foreign or mixed parentage, and 718,980 were native white of native parentage. The total is considerably lower than the actual number of persons who may correctly be called Mexican Americans, for there are many such persons who do not use Spanish habitually in their homes. There are actually between 2,500,000 and 3,000,000 persons in the United States who are Spanish-speaking in actuality or in derivation.

Today approximately half the Mexicans in the United States, over 1,000,000 of them, live in Texas, and they make up at least one-eighth of the total population of that state. A study of Texas made in 1942 and 1943 showed over 250,000 children of Mexican descent, 20.4 per cent of the total white scholastics. Thirty-six Texas counties had over 50 per cent Mexicans among their white scholastics; Zapata, Starr, and Webb counties had over 90 per cent Mexicans among their white scholastics. The percentage of Mexican scholastics in Laredo was 95.7 per cent, in El Paso 68.2 per cent, in San Antonio 58.6 per cent, in Corpus Christi 42.7 per cent, and in Houston 10.3 per cent.[3]

---

citizenship will be called *Mexicans*. Americans of non-Spanish heritage will be spoken of as *Anglos*, and where the reference is to both Mexicans and Mexican Americans, the more simple and inclusive terms *Mexicans* or *Spanish-speaking people* will be used.

[2] Sixteenth Census of the United States: 1940, Series P-12, No. 1, June, 1942, *Population of Spanish Mother Tongue: 1940*.

[3] Wilson Little, *Spanish-Speaking Children in Texas* (Austin, Texas: University of Texas Press, 1944), pp. 13-27.

During the last 30 years there has been a tendency
for many Mexicans to go elsewhere than to Texas. Although the total number in Texas does not seem to decrease, the numbers in California, Colorado, Arizona, and
states to the north of the Southwest have increased very
considerably. California has over 600,000 Mexicans,
mostly in the southern area; Los Angeles alone has about
125,000. The Spanish-speaking element in New Mexico,
some 250,000 strong, represents over 40 per cent of the
state's total population. Arizona has over 100,000 Mexicans who represent 20 per cent of that state's population.
Colorado also has over 100,000, located in the southern
Colorado river valleys, in Denver, and in the agricultural
area north of Denver. The 300,000 Spanish-speaking
population of New York is predominantly Puerto Rican
and will be discussed later. Denver ranks high in the list
of cities with large Mexican populations, particularly if
transients are included. Some 25,000 live in Chicago;
and Detroit, Gary, and Kansas City also have sizable
Mexican populations.[4] Since 1930 there has been hardly
a city of 25,000 population in either Texas or California
which has not had at least one hundred Mexicans. These
figures are indicative of the gradual urbanization of the
Spanish-speaking group, for over half of them now live,
at least semipermanently, in urban areas. Much of this
urban residence consists of using the city as a winter home
which is left in the spring and summer for migratory agricultural labor. Within the past twenty years, however,
there has been an increase in the industrialization of Mexican workers. In Chicago, for example, Mexicans first
appeared as track laborers, and later were employed in the
steel mills, the packing plants, and the tanneries. Their
number increased from about 3,800 in 1920 to about
25,000 in 1950.[5]

[4] Sixteenth Census of the United States, with some revision from later
estimates.

[5] Carey McWilliams, *North From Mexico* (New York: Lippincott,
1949), p. 184.

There is general agreement that the Mexican minority has a high death rate but a birth rate more than high enough to offset the death rate. Exact comparative figures are unavailable, for Texas, with the largest number of Mexicans, was not included in the birth and death registration area for a long time. Moreover, the population base for calculating Mexican rates has a tendency to shift so rapidly and so radically that such rates are neither strictly accurate nor strictly comparable with those of other groups. Woofter reports that in Los Angeles from 1916 to 1927 the Mexicans made up 8 per cent of the population and contributed 24 per cent of the excess of births over deaths. He suggests two major reasons for this high birth rate: (1) Mexicans, unlike most immigrants, commonly emigrate as "young" families, already at or in the child-bearing period and it is highly significant that often they made no attempt to limit the number of children since in agriculture children are an asset at a fairly early age; (2) They are predominantly Catholic, and they are predominantly of that group which, because of ignorance and lack of education, know little of contraception and lack sufficient regular income to put their little knowledge into effect.[6]

Immigration. The immigration of Mexicans, like all immigration, is the result of both attractive and expulsive forces. The chief attractive force has been and is still basically economic. Wage differentials have been so great in the two countries, especially for common labor, that many persons could make more money in three months in the United States than in a whole year in Mexico. The largest numbers of immigrants have come from the central and northern plateaus in the states of Michoacan, Jalisco, and Guanajuato. There most of the population is agri-

[6] T. J. Woofter, *Races and Ethnic Groups in American Life* (New York: McGraw-Hill, 1933), p. 16.

cultural, the birth rate is high, and the peon farm laborers have long been exploited on large, monopolistic land holdings. Wage rates before the revolution were as low as 25 cents a day, with no hope of advancement.[7] Inextricably interwoven with this purely economic attraction is family attraction, most commonly observable in cases where a successful immigrant urges other members of his family to come north to share the great opportunities. The first immigrants were foot-loose, adventurous young men; later came family men who sent for their families as the fabulous stories they had heard were partially realized. Although the immigrants were of all varieties of culture, literacy, religion, language, racial stock, and experience, they most typically were peons and *mestizos*, poorly educated, Catholic, without any special skills. Folklore, tradition, and custom played large roles in their lives, particularly since many of the elders were illiterate.

The expulsive forces have been more varied and less significant. They include political disorders and upheavals, religious disturbances, monotony, grinding poverty, and the tremendous obstacles the Mexicans encountered in attempting to advance themselves. These forces are difficult to measure for they happen to have coincided with periods of prosperity and high wages for labor in the United States. Awareness of the differentials in the two countries has often been the result of direct recruiting by labor agents representing railroads, factories, and large agricultural groups. The United States did not have a glutted labor market when European immigration was drastically curtailed by the Quota Act, hence any new labor demands of our expanding economy exerted pressure on Mexican laborers to enter. In 1913, large groups of Mexicans, as many as 2,000 at a time, were transported

[7] For the best study of sources and destinations of Mexican immigrants, see Manuel Gamio, *Mexican Immigration to the United States* (Chicago: University of Chicago Press, 1930), chap. ii.

by truck to the Imperial Valley. By 1920, half of the migratory laborers in the valley were Mexican; during 1924-30, almost 60,000 a year were brought in until by 1930 it was estimated that there were 250,000 Mexicans in California, who were liked and exploited by growers and merchants alike.[8] That the economic factor is of primary importance can be seen in the fact that when wages dropped and jobs disappeared, the great tide of Mexican immigration immediately ceased and became almost a mass exodus.

Between 1850 and 1900, immigration was largely a two-way traffic of shepherds, cowboys, ranch hands, and common laborers who did not think of themselves as emigrating; they went north to work just as they went east, west, and south, and it was incidental that they crossed an international border to work and recrossed it to return home. Neither government had any interest in this traffic. Such persons were not especially welcome, but they were too few in number to form a dangerous pool of cheap labor. Between 1900 and 1910 the tide began to swell; California's Mexican population quadrupled and the number in Kansas increased from less than 100 to almost 10,000. Somewhat later Texas, too, had a proportionately large increase. Between 1910 and 1930 the tide flowed ever faster. In 1900 Arizona had 14,171 Mexicans, by 1930 114,173; California's increase was from 8,086 to 368,013; New Mexico's Mexican population increased from 6,649 in 1900 to 59,340 in 1930; the increase in Texas was from 71,062 to 683,681. During the 1900 to 1930 wave of immigration, nearly 10 per cent of Mexico's adult population came to the United States.[9] To trace the story of Mexican immigration to the United States is to trace the rise of the great regional industries—railroads, mining,

[8] Carey McWilliams, *Factories in the Field* (New York: Little, Brown and Co., 1939), pp. 124-25.
[9] McWilliams, *North from Mexico*, p. 163.

citrus fruit, sugar beets, winter vegetables, cotton. The
flow of Mexican population into each state coincides with
its emerging development and prosperity.[10]

A study of Mexican immigrant families in Texas[11]
showed that most of them came from relatively small
towns in Mexico between 1910 and 1920. The men had
come in their late teens or twenties and the women mostly
in their teens. Somewhat fewer than half had been married before emigrating. While a good many of them came
as young adults, many others came as children with their
families. However, the major difference between Mexican immigration and that of other ethnic minorities in this
country is that the Mexicans can and do go back and forth
across the border. Most Mexican immigrants do not intend to become permanent residents of the United States;
many of them are engaged in seasonal work, and returning
home is normal for them. Mexicans do not come under
the Quota Law; if they meet the general requirements of
age, morality, literacy, health, self-support, etc., any number may enter, and any individual may enter as often as
he desires. At border cities like El Paso, considerable
numbers come over in the morning, work all day, and
return home at night. As a result, figures on Mexican
immigration are chaotic at best. Gamio,[12] using both Mexican and United States immigration figures, shows a great
many serious inconsistencies. In one six-year period alone
there was a difference of over 100,000 in the estimate of
the number who entered the United States, and a difference of over 450,000 in the number leaving the United

[10] Ruth D. Tuck, *Not with the Fist* (New York: Harcourt, Brace and
Co., 1946), p. 61. This source also contains, pp. 71-121, a composite life
history of "Juan Perez," a typical immigrant. While too long to reproduce
here, it is highly recommended as a case study.

[11] Marcus S. Goldstein, *Demographic and Bodily Changes in Descendants of Mexican Immigrants* (Austin, Texas: Institute of Latin-American
Studies, 1943).

[12] Gamio, *Mexican Immigration*, chap. i.

States. The Mexican count of returning immigrants consistently has been higher than the United States count of enterers, yet the Mexican population in the United States has consistently and steadily grown by more than its natural increase. The main explanation of such discrepancies lies in the very large number of Mexicans who have entered illegally. The border is long and difficult to police, so that it is probable that from 30 per cent to 50 per cent of Mexican immigrants have entered illegally.[13] Probably not many fewer than 2,500,000 Mexicans have entered the United States in the last 40 years and probably about 750,000 of them have remained permanently or for a considerable number of years. The high rate of illegal entry arose not only from the long, poorly patroled border and the desire of the Mexican to emigrate, but also from fear and ignorance of immigration laws, inability to meet the legal requirements, especially literacy, loss of time and expense involved in red tape, willingness of employers to hire "wetbacks,"[14] and particularly from the fact that the $18.00 fee is far too great for many immigrants to pay.[15] Mexican immigration of both types reached its peak in the middle twenties, over 100,000 a year, and then dwindled until 1930. During this period of high immigration there were periodic demands for the placing of Mexico under the Quota Act. Both the Box Bill (1925) and the Harris Bill (1926) were of this nature and would have limited immigration to 1,575 persons. The proponents of such bills were labor unions, social workers, and bigots, but they were defeated by the railroads and especially by the large agricultural interests who wanted, at the peak seasons,

[13] McWilliams, in *Factories in the Field*, p. 125, estimates that 80 per cent of the Mexicans in California entered illegally.

[14] *Wetback* is a term used on the border to indicate a Mexican who swam the Rio Grande instead of crossing legally over a bridge—in Spanish, *espaldas mojadas*.

[15] For an interesting novel on this illegal immigration, see Claud Garner, *Wet Back* (New York: Coward-McCann, 1947).

much peon labor which could and would return home during the remainder of the year. From 1930 to 1941 the number of immigrants was very small, averaging about 2,500 legal entries a year. This precipitous decline from the twenties would be easily understandable in view of our economic conditions during that period, but in addition, restrictions were tightened. The Mexican government, alarmed over the loss of so many workers, imposed more stringent restrictions on leaving Mexico. The United States, for her part, was much alarmed over the entrance of potential unemployed. While no major changes were made in the laws, immigration officers were ordered to enforce all existing laws to the letter, including all the "fine print." Such strict interpretation meant that only a relatively small number of those who desired it were actually permitted legal entry. The requirement of the written promise of two separate jobs was itself enough to bar most immigrants.

As early as 1921 the Mexican government was concerned over the loss of its citizens, and instituted efforts at repatriation. Special rates were made on railroads, steamships were chartered, and thousands of Mexicans returned home. More thousands, however, continued to cross the border northward. In 1929-30, the Mexican government again tried repatriation, with even more success, settling many repatriates on newly colonized government land. From that time to the present the repatriation program has been a continuing one, with dwindling success. The chief impetus for the return of some 300,000 to 400,000 Mexicans came, however, from the United States. Having lived from hand to mouth even in prosperous times, the majority had no reserves to fall back on when the depression occurred, and had to choose between returning to Mexico and going on relief. Many returned to Mexico and many more were returned at United States' expense.

Under the threat of being denied relief payments and on the promise of free transportation and food to the border, over 100,000 persons were returned to Mexico. The social agencies of most cities felt that it was much cheaper to pay the alien's transportation back than to support him, so that such informal deportation became almost standard procedure in the Southwest and Great Plains regions, despite the opposition of the large agricultural interests there.

Since 1940, the number of illegal Mexican immigrants has again increased, and exceeds the number entering legally. During the war years wages in the United States went up faster than the cost of living, while the Mexican cost of living went up faster than wages, and in 1948 was 300 per cent of the 1939 index. In 1946, the Mexican government admitted that at least 119,000 Mexicans were illegally in United States border areas, some 100,000 in Texas. These 119,000 became "legally admitted" by international agreement, legalized by signing contracts with employers at prevailing wages. These in the Lower Rio Grande Valley were set at 25 cents per hour and at up to 65 cents per hour in southern California.[16] Legal entries number about 10,000 a year of late, but the number of illegal entrants is considerably larger. The commissioner of immigration and naturalization has stated, "Several thousand of these illegal entrants are being apprehended in the United States each week and returned to their homes."[17] Since the fall of 1948 the Immigration Bureau has begun to tighten its operations under the cloud of a possible future depression. During 1949 some 3,000 to 4,000 were deported each month from California alone. According to the Los Angeles *Times* of September 22,

[16] Pauline R. Kibbe, "The American Standard—For all Americans," *Common Ground*, X (Autumn, 1949), 19-27.

[17] Watson B. Miller, "Administering Our Immigration Laws," *Annals of the American Academy of Political and Social Science*, CCLXII (March, 1949), 184.

1947, in 1946 over 66,000 illegal entrants were deported along the far western section of the border. At El Paso, Texas, for the fiscal year ending July 1, 1948, arrests made by the Border Patrol totaled 22,544; in the following six months, there were 20,979 arrests. During the harvest season between 20,000 and 40,000 persons enter illegally each month. As a rule, they go to work fairly close to the border; it was estimated that in 1948 about 90 per cent of the cotton in the Rio Grande Valley around El Paso was picked by wetbacks. Because of large numbers and because of the threat of deportation, wages are very low. Ordinary agricultural labor in 1947 and 1948 was paid 10 cents—25 cents an hour, with an agreed wage for cotton picking of from $1.50 to $2.00 per hundred pounds, as compared to $3.00 elsewhere.

The report of the President's Commission on Migratory Labor[18] indicates that, in the years immediately preceding 1944, wetback deportation averaged about 19,000 a year; in 1944 it went up to 25,000, and to 565,000 in 1950. The commission estimated that of one million Mexican agricultural laborers in the United States in 1949, 40,000 were wetbacks. One cause of this invasion is to be found in the increase in Mexico's population—from 16,500,000 in 1930 to 25,500,000 in 1950. At the same time, Mexican economy has remained primarily agricultural, with the volume of crops restricted by lack of mechanization and scarcity of water. The cost of living index, with 1939 as 100, stood at 354 in June, 1950. In October, 1949, the median salary for agricultural workers in the frontier zones near the United States was 65 cents a day and in the interior about 38 cents a day. The frontier zone in Mexico has experienced a great economic expansion; for example, the production of cotton in the Matamoros area has increased from 46,000 bales in 1939 to

[18] An excellent summary of this report is to be found in *Ciencias Sociales*, II (Oct.-Dec., 1951), 85 ff.

300,000 bales in 1949. The population in the border areas has increased, too. Between 1940 and 1950 Mexicali increased 240 per cent, Tijuana 259 per cent, Cuidad Juarez 149 per cent, Nogales 78 per cent, Nuevo Laredo 99 per cent, and Matamoros 179 per cent. Without exception the affected areas have been unable to absorb economically the migration to them. For example, when 25,000 cotton pickers were needed recently in the Matamoro area, 60,000 were available. In short, much of the cause for the wetback invasion of the Southwest can be traced to internal conditions in Mexico, where large reserves of potential wetbacks are being accumulated in border areas unable to absorb them. At the same time, just across the border in the United States, economic expansion has created new needs for manual labor, agricultural and otherwise, along with increasing difficulty in securing such labor north of the border. The recommendations of the commission include: (1) greater vigilance of frontier officers (about 25 per cent of the wetbacks are deported); (2) greater power for immigration officials to investigate the places of employment of wetbacks; (3) stronger regulation against those encouraging illegal immigration; (4) facilitation and increase of legal contract labor; (5) soliciting aid from Mexico in policing the frontier and in keeping large numbers of manual workers from the frontier states.

Social and economic conditions of wetbacks are worse than the low norm for other Mexicans in these areas. Wetbacks have no financial resources, are dependent upon their employers, are frightened of Anglo contact, and do not understand Anglo customs; virtual peonage sometimes occurs. According to the study of Saunders and Leonard,[19] about one-half of them come from the states of Nuevo Leon, Guanajuato, and San Luis Potosi, and half the re-

[19] Lyle Saunders and Olen E. Leonard, *The Wetback in the Lower Rio Grande Valley of Texas* (Austin, Texas: University of Texas Publications, 1951).

mainder from Jalisco and Michoacan. Over half were young bachelors, the vast majority had been agricultural laborers in Mexico, and almost all expected to return to Mexico after two or three months, having come over only to get the "high" wages (around 20 cents an hour) during the harvest season. The cheap new wetback labor causes earlier residents, possibly once wetbacks themselves, to move northward. Here they compete with Anglos, other Mexicans and Negroes, which groups, in turn, are pushed farther north. The wage scale becomes progressively higher as one moves away from the border—up to 100 per cent higher—but Mexican migrants, wetback or not, have an unwilling tendency to depress wages as they move northward. Not all wetbacks enter agricultural labor. It is estimated that, in 1949, 6,000 of the 21,000 persons in the labor force in the city of El Paso were illegal entrants. Unions, of course, have strongly opposed the entrance and employment of wetbacks, but this influence has been effectively offset by farmers and farm organizations interested in cheap seasonal labor.

Living conditions of wetbacks are unbelievably poor and primitive, but nothing has been done about them except that in Texas in the early 1940's labor center camps were set up with federal funds and administered by the Texas Agricultural and Mechanical College Extension Service. These camps were uniformly well administered, and there were 63 at the peak, but when federal funds were withdrawn the program collapsed; some camps were taken over by counties, by cities, or by private individuals, and the remainder were abandoned.[20] At best, the life of a wetback is not an enviable one: he receives the very lowest of wages, has no job security, constantly fears arrest

[20] The above material on recent wetback immigration was drawn chiefly from Art Leibson, "The Wetback Invasion," *Common Ground*, X (Autumn, 1949), 11-19, and Hart Stillwell, "The Wetback Tide," *Common Ground*, X (Summer, 1949). 3-14.

and deportation, is likely to be looked upon with considerable disfavor by the resident Mexicans, cannot complain of mistreatment, and has little chance for assimilation.

The illegal migrant is subject to deportation for the first five years he is in the United States. After this time he will not be deported unless it is found that he was and is a member of an excludable class. The general policy is that if he could have been a legal immigrant had he tried, he is permitted to remain. If he has been or is in trouble with the law, he will be deported, but he may remain, even as a public charge, if the causes arose after entry. An immigrant who came in before July 1, 1924, may pay an immigration fee of $18.00 and be considered a legal immigrant.

Illegal immigration may be expected to continue to provide a large proportion of all Mexican immigrants for some time, for legal immigration is somewhat difficult due to the present policies of both the Mexican and United States governments. We have had a number of years of successful experience with short-term, government-controlled contract labor, and it seems likely that this program will again come into prominence when needed. Agricultural interests still want large bodies of cheap labor at harvest time, but do not particularly desire permanent immigration. In short, the pressure of Mexico's high birth rate on her limited resources will, as long as it continues, create expulsive forces which will result in both legal and illegal emigration of Mexicans to the United States. Mexican immigration was a trickle until 1910, a wave from 1910 until 1930, and has been since then, and probably will continue to be, a sizable if fluctuating stream. There can be no question but that this immigration is serious for the Mexican Americans and Spanish Americans in the border areas; for them it continues poverty by keeping wages very low, it retards assimilation, and it contributes to discrimination and to ethnic hostility.

Migratory Labor. The existence of a reservoir of low-paid labor over the border has been one of the major factors in the growth of commercial truck farming and large-scale agriculture in the Southwest and some areas of the Great Plains. So efficient was this interaction of supply and demand that in Texas alone, where there were some 226,000 Mexicans in 1910, the number had increased to 1,250,000 by 1950. This group still continues to be made up largely of migratory agricultural laborers who follow the seasonal crops. They do the harvesting of truck crops in the late winter and early spring, work in the cotton fields during the summer, or move north into the Great Plains to work on sugar beets. "Migration has become a way of life with the Mexicans, who have in turn become accepted as a stable source of labor by growers of cotton, vegetables, and other crops . . . as well as by sugar beet growers."[21]

Paul S. Taylor reports a case history which may well be typical.[22] The family came in at Laredo, Texas. Just north of there is the Winter Garden, where the onion harvest was on, so the family worked until the harvest ended. Thence they went to San Antonio where they were unable to support themselves. Several members then got temporary work in a cottonseed-oil refinery in a central Texas town, after which the family continued north to Fort Worth. There they met a labor contractor who shipped them out to the sugar-beet fields in Montana. When this work ran out they followed the beet season to Wyoming. The winter was spent in Denver with only occasional odd jobs for support. The next season they worked in the beet fields in Colorado, ending the season with $15.00 and an old car. Heading back to Texas they went broke at Raton, New Mexico, where the father worked in a coal mine for a year. They were able to save enough to get them back

[21] Selden C. Menefee, *Mexican Migratory Workers of South Texas* (Washington: Government Printing Office, 1941), pp. x-xi.
[22] Paul S. Taylor, "Mexicans North of the Rio Grande," *Survey*, LXVI (May 1, 1931), 138.

to the Winter Garden in Texas, where they went to work in the onion fields, to begin the cycle again.[23]

The case above is by no means atypical, for the Mexicans and Mexican Americans are the greatest migrant labor force in America. A study of Crystal City, Texas, Mexican families showed that when the spinach was cut, 19 out of 20 families migrated to work on other crops.[24] A scattering of tenant farmers may be found in south and west Texas, southern California or Colorado, but such stability is rarely achieved. With the exception of New Mexico, previously discussed, the Mexican is everywhere and in general a farm laborer, not a farm operator or factory worker. He works on onions, spinach, tomatoes, melons, citrus fruit, and cotton in Texas, on vegetables, fruit, melons and cotton in California and Arizona, and on sugar beets in Colorado, Utah, Wyoming, California, Montana, Nebraska, Minnesota, Michigan, and the Dakotas. Only in the cotton areas of south central and southwest Texas has he been able to become a tenant farmer, replacing the Negro. As migratory laborers the Mexicans are well liked. The California Fact-Finding Commission[25] found that 35.7 per cent of the farmers preferred Mexicans, 20.5 per cent whites, 14.8 per cent Japanese, 7.1 per cent Filipinos, and 7.4 per cent others. Not unimportant in this popularity was the fact that wages paid Mexicans tended to be slightly lower than those paid to other groups; docility and nonunionization were also considered favorable factors.

[23] A number of good case histories may be found in Appendix A of Amber A. Warburton, Helen Wood, and Marian M. Crane, *The Work and Welfare of Children of Agricultural Laborers in Hidalgo County, Texas* (Children's Bureau Publication 298 [Washington: U. S. Department of Labor, 1943]). Louis Adamic, *From Many Lands* (New York: Harper and Brothers, 1940), pp. 237-84, also contains a long case history of a Mexican immigrant boy.

[24] Menefee, *Mexican Migratory Workers*, pp. 19-26; Carey McWilliams, *Ill Fares the Land* (New York: Little, Brown and Co., 1942), p. 116.

[25] Reported in Woofter, *Races and Ethnic Groups in American Life* (New York: McGraw-Hill, 1933), pp. 109-10.

By 1916 the Great Western Sugar company began to import Mexicans, first from southern Colorado, then from New Mexico, Arizona, and Texas; for many years it maintained recruiting offices in the larger cities of that area which sent up thousands of laborers each year. These officers distributed handbills even more widely, and paid transportation one way if necessary, importing workers by the tens of thousands. Each year a number of workers remained at the end of the season and more and more voluntarily made the trip north, so that gradually labor recruitment became less important. Efforts were made to retain the workers in northern Colorado by offering them free rent, grocery credit, and colonization projects, while wages were kept low by continually importing new workers to keep the supply greater than the demand.[26]

A nationwide survey showed that two-thirds of all sugar-beet field workers were Mexicans and Mexican Americans.[27] The farmers like them as field laborers because they are quiet, hard workers who keep to themselves, because their large families contain several workers each, and because most of them disappear in the winter to their homes in Texas and other Southwestern states. The Mexicans accept this type of work because the wages in beets are higher than those paid in cotton and other crops raised in the Southwest. Beet work is definitely seasonal but lasts longer than that for most crops. The worker normally contracts for a given amount of acreage, i.e., a man ten acres, a woman seven, and a child less. There are four main operations: (1) "blocking," chopping out overcrowded plants from the rows of beets so as to leave a tuft of beets every ten or twelve inches; (2) "thinning," pulling out by hand all but the strongest plant in each tuft;

[26] Carey McWilliams, *Factories in the Field*, pp. 110-14.
[27] Elizabeth S. Johnson, *Welfare of Families of Sugar-Beet Laborers* (Washington: United States Department of Labor Children's Bureau, 1939). p. 13.

(3) "hoeing" once or twice a summer to keep the soil loose and free from weeds; and (4) "pulling" the beets at harvest, after they have been loosened by a tractor-drawn lifter, cutting off the tops and piling up the beets. Uusually payment is made, by the acre, after each operation. The average job ties the laborer to the land for five to seven months, during which time he actually works from sixty to ninety days. He usually has a house of poor quality furnished free, but he rarely has opportunity for supplemental labor during the season. A bonus or a hold-back payable at the end of the season is used to encourage the worker to remain for the entire season to finish the crop. Once the grower finds satisfactory workers, he encourages them to return to him each year so that it will be unnecessary for him to seek laborers. A minority of workers still work under a labor-contracting system by which a Mexican agent undertakes to supply labor to one or more growers.[28] Wages in beets have been better than in most other types of agricultural labor, but before World War II the per capita income of beet workers unable to supplement that income was about a hundred dollars a year, which was below the official government minimum cash budget, but far above that of comparable families studied in San Antonio and California.[29]

Between 1920 and 1940 average wages for Mexican agricultural laborers were about 18 cents an hour; the peak was about 35 cents in 1928 and the low about 15 cents in 1934. Since the war, wages have risen considerably, and are set by government-sponsored hearings. For 1950 the minimum wage in beets was 60 cents and 65 cents per hour, with a bonus for extra work. Because much of such labor is necessary for beet production, every large city of the Southwest has labor contractors—usually unlicensed and extralegal—who serve as the middlemen between

---

[28] Menefee, *Mexican Migratory Workers*, pp. 19-26, and Carey McWilliams, *Ill Fares the Land*, p. 116.
[29] Menefee, *Mexican Migratory Workers*, pp. 19-26, 37.

supply and demand. Very commonly such contractors load as many persons as possible into an old truck and drive them north, where there may or may not be work awaiting them. Such trucks are not commonly noticed on the highways, as the extralegal contractors find it safer to drive at night over the less used roads.[30]

Despite the fact that sugar-beet work is looked upon with favor by most migratory Mexican laborers, it has been considered for fifteen years to be a serious social and economic problem by those who study it, and the large sugar companies have received considerable verbal and written castigation as a result. It is therefore heartening to note that during and after World War II conditions improved markedly. Real wages have not increased much, but the Great Western Sugar Company, for example, has shown others the way by establishing, in 1949, a model distributing-center camp at Fort Lupton, Colorado. Through this camp pass some 15,000 workers a year for placement on individual farms. While waiting assignment the families are fed and housed free, given chest X-rays, inoculations and other medical care, and recreational facilities. What charges are made are charged to the ultimate employer, not the laborer. This camp was one of those constructed by the government for migratory workers during the war, but the only one to the author's knowledge now being used as a distributing center.

Along with sugar beets in importance to Mexican migratory labor is cotton, and the most important state for such labor is Texas. Texas normally grows about one-fourth of the nation's cotton, and three-fourths of Texas's migratory cotton pickers are Mexican. They mostly work in south, south central, and western Texas, since picking in the other areas is done chiefly by local labor. In the earlier days a contract system was used centering in a *jefe* who made agreements with growers and served as business

[30] Cf. McWilliams, *Factories in the Field*, pp. 264-71.

agent for his workers. He supervised the weighing and
hauling of the cotton and collected the amount due the
worker from the grower.[31] As the workers learn their
way around and are able to furnish their own transportation they leave this system, since it is commonly charged
that contractors collect too much rebate and are not respon-
sive to complaints. The system has by no means disappeared as yet, for the *jefe* speaks English, has initiative,
and has transportation—all three of which are important.
In the area of extensive farms, a large truck may carry 30
to 40 workers who stay a few days on each farm, camping
anywhere, and then move on. Often the group is made
up of three or four large families with collateral relations.
Despite its abuses, the contract system does tend to help
organize an otherwise very chaotic labor market. Half or
more of the cotton pickers no longer use contractors, traveling greater distances, staying a little longer at each farm,
and stopping at the smaller farms which a large labor
contractor would skip. Greater facilities at United States
Employment Service local offices make the proper distribution of such labor much more satisfactory than before
World War II.

Migratory labor in the Texas cotton fields differs from
that in many other states because it does not come from
outside the state and does not have a very wide range of
employment. Almost 500,000 Mexicans, who make up
75 per cent of Texas's migratory labor, harvest over half
its cotton crop.[32] The season is short enough that a truck-
load of workers, moving rather rapidly, can catch all the
major harvests. Workers on the "big swing" start about
July 1 in the southern tip, move a month later to the south
central and coastal areas, move west about September 1 to

[31] Cf. Max Handman, "Economic Reasons for the Coming of the Mexican Immigrant," *American Journal of Sociology*, XXXV (Jan., 1930),
601-11.
[32] For the most complete study of Mexican labor in Texas, see Paul S.
Taylor, *An American-Mexican Frontier: Neuces County, Texas* (Chapel
Hill, N. C.: University of North Carolina Press, 1934).

central Texas and then about October 1 arrive at the western cotton area, departing about December 1 to return to southern Texas for the vegetable and produce-crop work after being gone from eight to twenty weeks. Possibly half make the complete circle; others join the army for a few weeks as it moves, and then drop out to return home.[33] Where possible these workers prefer to drive their own cars. Probably about half do so; the others ride with friends or relatives, pay their way on trucks, or travel with a labor contractor. Much disorganization naturally occurs in such a labor market. No group of growers ever seems to have enough labor, for "enough" really means a labor surplus great enough to bring down wages. To discourage the transporting of Texas labor outside the state, the legislature in 1929 enacted the Emigrant Agent Act requiring any person or firm sending labor out of the state to pay an annual state tax of $1,000, execute a bond of $5,000, and pay an additional graduated tax to the county of operation. An example of the problems encountered in trying to regulate the movements of migratory laborers is the case reported by Menefee in which the Farm Placement Service "received a long distance telephone call stating that farmers in a certain community were in need of 2,000 cotton pickers. An employee of the Service hurried to the scene. He asked the names of growers who were most in need and was told that 'every farmer in that trade territory was seriously in need of labor.' Unable to secure any specific information . . . he made an immediate and thorough survey of the labor situation in the community. He found that there was actual need of only 85 cotton pickers."[34]

Much the same situation has existed in the cotton-growing area of Arizona. In 1920 Arizona cotton growers spent $300,000 recruiting pickers from outside the state.

[33] Cf. Carey McWilliams, *Ill Fares the Land*, pp. 231 ff.
[34] Menefee, *Mexican Migratory Workers*, p. 31, quoting from Farm Placement Service, *Survey of Farm Placement in Texas, 1936 and 1937*, p. 45.

By 1937 the same number of workers, still mostly Mexican, but including some stranded "Okies," could be recruited for only $900 by the use of such small advertisements as the one below from the November 11, 1937, Santa Fe *El Nuevo Mexicano*.[35]

NECESITAMOS
RECOGEDORES
DE ALGODON

se necesitan
500 FAMILIAS
Millares De Acres De Algodon Blanco Coma La
Nieve. En La Vecinedad
de Phoenix y Coolidge,
Arizona
Los Cultivadores Pagan
$1.75 POR CIEN LIBRAS
DE FIBRA LARGA Y 85c
POR FIBRA CORTA
Buenos Campos, Cabanas y
Alfaneques Gratis
La Recolleccion Durara
Hasta Enero
Dias Calientes, Secas y Resplandecientes en el Otono
e Invierno
Buen Trabajo Seguro y
Estable Si Viene Pronto
FARM LABOR SERVICE
No. 28 West Jefferson Street
Phoenix, Arizona

[35] Reported in Malcolm Brown and Orin Cassmore, *Migratory Cotton Pickers in Arizona* (Washington, U. S. Government Printing Office, 1939). See also Wallace Stegner, *One Nation* (New York: Houghton-Mifflin, 1945), p. 96.

Next to beet and cotton growers, as employers of Mexican labor, rank large truck gardeners, mostly in Texas. The onion harvest begins in April in the Texas Winter Garden and continues into July in northern Texas. Most beet workers must leave before the onion harvest is well under way, but cotton and onions may be combined satisfactorily. The Winter Garden grows huge amounts of spinach, onions, cabbage, beans, tomatoes, and other truck crops. These are harvested by Mexicans, only a minority of whom are truly migratory. Most of the workers live in the shack towns of the relatively near-by border cities. For such employment most Mexicans work under contractors in groups of 200 to 250. They must be available for work each morning, but they may work all day, three hours, or not at all. Despite such conditions, the workers who live in the Winter Garden area are a select group having much more work available than those living farther north. A study of Mexicans in this Winter Garden area showed that 9 out of 10 did some migrating. Only 1 in 40 had no unemployment during the year, 1 in 3 had been unemployed two months or more, and 1 in 8 had been unemployed more than half the year.[36]

Warburton, Wood, and Crane, in their study of moderately stable agricultural workers in Hidalgo County, Texas, found that during the year 1940 these families had a median cash income from all sources of only $350 to provide for their large households, averaging 6.6 persons. This was considerably less than the minimum annual income estimated by the Texas Social Welfare Association to be necessary to maintain relief families, averaging only 4.2 members, at a level of health and decency. Yet very few of the families had received any assistance from public or private agencies during the year.

Needless to say, this whole way of life has very serious

[36] Menefee, *Mexican Migratory Workers*, p. 15.

repercussions on the children. More than ¼ of the children aged 6 to 9 years, and ⅖ of those between 10 and 14 worked at some time during the preceding year. Nearly all the boys and girls over 14 were regular members of the family working force. While the younger children sometimes worked only during the summer and early fall, the older children generally worked whenever work was available, regardless of whether school was in session or not. Of the 837 boys and girls in the study who were between 6 and 16, not quite 60 per cent were enrolled in school, and about 20 per cent had never been enrolled in any school. Less than 6 per 100 youths 16 or 17 years of age were still in school. Most of the boys and girls who had reached 14, and many who were younger, had permanently withdrawn from school owing chiefly to their families' need for their earnings; ⁹⁄₁₀ of the boys and girls who had been to school were overage for their grade.[37]

The United States Department of Agriculture has formulated very comprehensive recommendations for improving the condition of migratory laborers. These include the establishment of adequate child labor and minimum wage laws, the establishment of regulated labor camps, extension of Social Security and Workmen's Compensation to include this group, acquainting local communities and the general public with the value of and plight of migratory workers, procedures for the maintenance of satisfactory employer-employee relations and advance determination and accurate description of period of employment, number of workers needed, nature of work, wages, housing, etc., to secure more efficient recruitment and placement of migrant workers.[38]

Wherever he goes the Mexican is cheap labor. Alien

[37] Warburton, *et al.*, *Work and Welfare*, pp. 4-16.
[38] Federal Interagency Committee on Migrant Labor, *Migrant Labor . . . A Human Problem* (Washington: United States Department of Agriculture, March, 1947), pp. 7-13.

status makes it more difficult for him to secure steady employment. He has shown only moderate interest in organized labor, and as an individual bargainer—often hungry—he has been no match for shrewd, experienced employers. There is small stimulus to try to advance. Mexicans, like other minority groups, tend to be marginal workers, the last to be hired and the first to be fired.

Contract Labor. During the early war years there was a great shortage of agricultural labor. Previous supplies of such labor had been drawn off by industrial employment, by the armed forces, and by the withdrawal of woman and child labor where the husband and father alone was now making an income sufficient to support the family. At the same time there were greater demands than ever for agricultural produce, and generally superior climatic conditions were producing large yields. It was obvious that workers from some other countries were needed, with Mexico and the Caribbean Islands the logical sources. Since it was also obvious that a co-ordinated and planned program would be more efficient than haphazard immigration, a treaty was negotiated between Mexico and the United States. This agreement provided that Mexican workers would be gathered, examined, and processed by the Mexican government. For those hired by railroads, the employer paid transportation from point of contract back again to point of contract. These workers were hired for 180 days, and could be rehired for periods of 90 days to the limit of 6 months. Housing cost railroad workers nothing, and food was free every working day. Agricultural workers had their transportation paid to the border by the Mexican government, and from the border to the work and back to the border by the United States government. Transportation within the United States was paid by the employer, ranging from about $10.00 to $150.00 per man, depending on distance. In both types of work, individual contracts were executed between the worker and the United States government, and then between the government and the employers. Until July, 1943, this program was in charge of the Farm Security Administration, and after that time of the War Food Administration. From 1943 to 1947 the federal government spent $120,000,000 on this program, using some 361,500 workers, only a few thousand of whom were not Mexicans. It is estimated that these laborers harvested crops worth $432,000,000 in 1944 alone. They saved crops in many areas where otherwise only partial harvests would have been possible, and were also employed by over 30 different railroads.

The individual contracts provided that: the employer guarantee employment for 75 per cent of the worker's time exclusive of Sundays; prevailing wages be paid for a workday of not less than eight and no more than twelve hours; the worker be entitled to full protection of United States labor laws and workmen's compensation insurance, and be issued a Social Security number; there should be no discrimination because of race, creed, color, or national origin, and the worker might make any purchases he wished wherever he wished; shelter facilities owned by the employer be available without charge (other shelter to be arranged for by the employer and paid for by the worker); workers have the right to organize with other Mexican nationals, but strikes and lockouts be prohibited; 10 per cent of all earnings be deposited by the employer to the worker's account in the Bank of Mexico. Since the workers received reasonably rigid health examinations in Mexico, the employer was usually expected to care for health needs of the workers. Because much of the work was done in gangs, it was usually convenient for the employer to see that the men were all fed together. Reasonable charges for such food were permissible. Employers arranged through the WFA for the number of persons they wished and their dates of arrival. The peak year was 1945, in which some 120,000 contract workers were used.

After 1946 regulations were relaxed. Often workers were processed on the Mexican side, walked over the bridge, and were loaded into trucks by contractors. The 10 per cent was still deducted, but was given to the worker in the form of a cashier's check which could not be cashed until stamped by Mexican immigration officials. The contract laborers went chiefly to large growers or corporations, who were responsible for them and who were required to forfeit a bond if the worker did not return to Mexico at the end of the contract period. There was a continued drop in the efficiency of the operation of the program during 1947, and as of January 1, 1948, Mexico terminated the agreement because of "lack of co-operation" of United States immigration officials. Mexico charged that her workers had no protection except as contract laborers, but that large agricultural interests were influencing the Immigration Bureau to permit all types of persons to enter; hence she was stopping the contract labor supply completely.[39] These charges were true in part, yet in 1946, on the western border alone, the Immigration Service apprehended 66,000 wetbacks and returned them to Mexico. The number of workers recruited for agricultural employment was: 1942—4,200; 1943—52,100; 1944—62,200; 1945—120,000; 1946—32,000; 1947—55,000.

Since 1948 the Mexican contract-labor agreements have been periodical. As of August, 1951, the agreement was that such laborers would be employed not less than six weeks and not more than six months, that they would receive the local "going wage," that they could not be used where a sufficiency of labor already existed, and that the workers would not go where there was racial discrimi-

[39] *Border Trends*, Southwest Area Office, Unitarian Service Committee, October, 1948, p. 36.

nation. Within the following two months about 100,000 contract laborers crossed the border, despite the active opposition of the Agricultural Laborers Union (AFL). In September of 1951 the agreement was suspended on a charge that some contract laborers were being fed dog food, but this was settled and the agreement reinstated.

In general the treatment of contract workers has been reasonably good. From the beginning Mexico refused to certify contract workers for Texas because of the traditional treatment of Mexicans in that state; before the program was finished Arkansas and Mississippi were also black-listed. This was not a typical pattern, however, and relatively few incidents occurred. In general the contract workers behaved themselves well, impressed employers and townspeople with their courtesy and willingness to work, and responded in kind to the occasional programs or picnics put on for them in the small towns in which they worked.[40] Undoubtedly the fact that as transient workers they were not a threat to the local labor supply had some bearing on their good treatment. Almost all the contract workers returned to Mexico at the expiration of their time. A few were willing to sacrifice their 10 per cent and "got lost," but they were an insignificant percentage, as were those who returned to Mexico and then came back as regular immigrants. Although the program had many defects, particularly after it was taken from the hands of the Farm Security Administration and given to the War Food Administration (i.e., the farm associations and big growers), it was a notable advance over the World War I experience. Stripped of technicalities, it was a new phase of the old search for cheap, unorganized mass labor, but it did show the superiority, for almost everyone concerned, of planned over unplanned immigration. As Wallace Stegner[41] says:

[40] One foreman told the author, "When they told me I'd have a crew of Mex's, I didn't like it, and was going to carry a gun to the field with me. After I'd worked them for a week, I wouldn't take any other kind of crew—they're swell fellows."

[41] Wallace Stegner, One Nation, p. 97.

The nationals themselves have been friendly, cooperative, generally pleased with America. The vital work they have done, and their own good behavior, have helped reduce the prejudice against Mexicans in many areas. . . . On the whole, the supervised borrowing of Mexican labor has been a conspicuous success.

Nonagricultural Economic Aspects. As a group, Mexican Americans have been agricultural rather than industrial workers. The first major nonagricultural opening came in 1921 when the Santa Fe Railroad announced it was replacing all Anglo workers with Mexicans as section hands in the state of Arizona. Now about half of all railroad-track laborers west and south of Chicago are Mexicans.[42] At other nonagricultural work, the Mexican immigrant was not very well liked. He was accused of being lazy and undependable, which he may have appeared to be. Actually, the better explanation is that the Mexican immigrant was accustomed to work by natural units of labor, building a fence, plowing a field, plastering an adobe house; he had difficulty in fitting himself into an impersonal schedule, working by the hour at someone else's rate of speed—using a whole new set of work habits.

Almost everywhere the Mexican worker has had to accept jobs in the unskilled category because of discrimination, ignorance, and actual lack of any skill which could be utilized in urban American culture. An illustration is the pecan-shelling industry studied by Menefee and Cassmore. In 1938 this industry employed some 10,000 persons, mostly Mexicans, in San Antonio. For exclusively hand labor, the wages averaged 5 cents to 8 cents an hour, and about $2.75 a week.[43] When ordered to pay the Fair Labor Standards Act minimum wages of 25 cents an hour, 80 per cent of the industry closed down. One interviewee who managed a pecan-shelling plant and was a self-con-

[42] Cf. Beatrice Griffith, *American Me* (Boston: Houghton-Mifflin Co., 1948), pp. 121-23.
[43] Seldon C. Menefee and Orin C. Cassmore, *The Pecan Shellers of San Antonio* (Washington: Government Printing Office, 1940), p. xvii.

fessed "authority," said if Mexicans were given the minimum wage they would work only three days a week because they would have all the money they wanted. At that very time over a thousand Mexican pecan shellers were docilely submitting to a major speed-up—so feared and hated by unions—in order to keep their five-and-a-half-day-week jobs at minimum wages.[44] Because of the abysmally low wages available, many pecan shellers worked as migrant agricultural laborers during the season. A fairly typical case was that of Manual Juarez, a widower, who had six children at home. In May, 1938, he left his pecan-shelling job, took the younger children out of school, and drove in his 1926 Model T Ford to the cotton fields near Corpus Christi, where the crop was rumored to be good. However, thousands of other Mexican families had also heard the same rumor, which was an exaggeration; and in 45 days the five members of the family who worked (ranging upward from Juanita, aged 10) managed only 3 days of work and earned only $10.00. In mid-July they left for Lamesa, in west Texas. It took them 8 days to cover the 650 miles, and when they arrived they found that the crop was no better than the one at Corpus Christi. They stayed at Lamesa 65 days, but earned only $18.00. Some of the other families with whom they were traveling were more fortunate, and by pooling their resources the several families were able to get enough to eat. In October Manuel borrowed money for gasoline to get home on but ran out of both gasoline and money about 15 miles from San Antonio. Hitchhiking into the city, he persuaded a friend with an automobile to tow his car in. He sold the car for $5.00 cash and a $5.00 grocery order, and rented a two-room shack for his family of seven for 50 cents a week. Before he could get back to work shelling pecans, however, the plants were closed down, and Manuel was forced to apply for surplus commodities.[45]

[44] *Ibid.*, p. 51.   [45] *Ibid.*, p. 28.

In the Northern cities, the situation has never been as serious as that just depicted. In Chicago, Gary, and Detroit, Mexican Americans have been employed in steel mills, in meat packing, and in automobile manufacture for two decades. Although the AFL for twenty-five years had opposed Mexican labor (some early Mexican immigrants had been brought north as strikebreakers), the CIO welcomed all the Mexican laborers it could recruit. The AFL's policies have been somewhat liberalized as a result of this competition. Mexican ˙business and professional men have seldom profited greatly, for they have had to depend upon their compatriots for customers and clients. This has meant that some trained and sympathetic persons speaking their own language were available to the Mexicans, but the low economic level of the group has frustrated the growth of a professional and managerial class to serve them. A study of the situation in Los Angeles in 1942 showed the following occupational comparison:

OCCUPATIONAL STATUS OF MEXICANS, JEWS, AND ANGLOS: LOS ANGELES, 1942[46]

Occupation	Per cent of Mexicans	Per cent of Anglos	Per cent of Jews
Unskilled	55.	21.	5.
Semiskilled	10.5	11.	7.
Skilled	16.	21.5	18.5
Clerical	10.5	26.5	35.5
Managerial	3.5	6.5	18.
Professional	1.5	10.	14.5
Entertainment	2.5	3.	1.
Military Service	.5	.5	.5

As can be seen by the above table, the service facilities operated by the group for the group tend to be rather rudimentary. The number and diversity of services of-

[46] Adapted from Edward C. McDonogh, "Status Levels of the American Jews," *Sociology and Social Research*, XXXII (July-Aug., 1948), 944-53.

fered seem to be less adequate than those of Negroes or Orientals; many of these enterprises are marginal and functionally isolated from the mass economy. One need seek the reason for this no further than the limitation of market imposed by the isolation of the Mexican community, the deficiency of capital, and the dearth of personnel with technical and professional skills. It seems unlikely that any great progress will be made in the field of business until the group accumulates more capital, more technically trained personnel, and a higher degree of leadership able to cope with government on its various levels.[47]

Whether gained from agriculture or some other pursuit, the earnings of the Mexicans have been so low for the group as a whole that even before 1930 a large number were periodically in need of charity. With the coming of depression conditions, at least half the Mexican minority were on relief rolls at one time or another.[48] Not far from 100 per cent of the migratory agricultural laborers were so represented if they were in any way eligible as to residence.

This generally impoverished condition has been the historic pattern for the Mexican American population. Here and there are well-to-do merchants, respected doctors, judges and lawyers, college professors, and entertainers, but they are the exception. In December, 1941, the income of the median Mexican family in Los Angeles was about $790 a year, some $520 less than the government-recommended minimum for feeding and housing a family of five decently. With the coming of the wartime shortage of all kinds of labor on the West Coast, the eco-

[47] Cf. Leonard Broom and Eshref Shevsky, "Mexicans in the United States: A Problem in Social Differentiation," *Sociology and Social Research*, XXXVI (Jan.-Feb., 1952), 150-58.

[48] The novel *Tumbleweeds*, by Marta Roberts (New York: G. P. Putman's Sons, 1940), describes very well the experiences of a Mexican family with social welfare agencies, the reaction of the family to such agencies, and the problems such an agency faced in assisting this type of family.

nomic status of the Mexicans there improved somewhat. Family income increased sharply, partly because of increased wages, but more because of increased industrial employment, and even more because now two, three, or four members of the same family were able to secure employment. Unions began to tolerate or even welcome Mexicans as members, after a considerable period of virtual exclusion. Training programs helped many of them acquire skills, and the federal Fair Employment Practices Commission's activities helped them secure jobs comparable to their abilities. Everywhere, except possibly in Texas, the Mexican began to find more employment from such nonagricultural employers as meat-packing houses, canning factories, steel mills, textile mills, and all types of miscellaneous industries requiring unskilled and semiskilled labor.[49]

In Texas, particularly south and central Texas, even in the postwar years Mexican Americans show a higher proportion of unskilled and semiskilled workers than do Anglos. Their rather typical exclusion from unions and low level of education are significant factors in explaining this differential, but discrimination in employment is also a factor. State employment agencies may make a practice of calling employers for verification before sending out skilled workers, like clerks and typists, with Spanish names. Only a few private and governmental offices hire Mexican Americans without reservations or quotas so that, even if skilled, Mexican Americans have a limited possibility of being employed at their optimum level.[50]

Even the earnings of agricultural workers increased markedly. Wages for sugar-beet workers were and still are set in consultation with the government. In 1947 the

[49] Cf. Griffith, *American Me*, pp. 266-69.
[50] Forest Burr Crain, *The Occupational Distribution of Spanish-name People in Austin, Texas* (Master's thesis, University of Texas, 1948), pp. 74-75.

average earning per worker, which represented 60 per cent of his season's earnings, was $383.[51] This represented, for a family of three workers, earnings quite adequate for decent living during the season. Unfortunately, not all families had three workers, and even more unfortunately, these families had to provide for living costs after the season was over. Earnings adequate for four months are totally inadequate when stretched over twelve.

Chicago has the largest concentration of Mexicans outside the Southwest. There the vast majority work in steel mills, in meat-packing plants, or on the railroads. As steelworkers they are mostly in the unskilled and semiskilled categories; of the Carnegie-Illinois Steel Company's 18,000 workers, some 4,000 are Mexicans. Some 1,000 to 2,000 are employed in the meat-packing industry, chiefly as unskilled laborers. Those employed by the railroads work mostly as section hands and as laborers in the car repair shops; although mostly unskilled, the Mexicans include some skilled workers and some foremen. Among the 20,000 to 25,000 Mexicans in Chicago, as of 1948, there were 3 physicians, 2 dentists, 6 teachers, 6 engineers, 10 laboratory technicians, 15 welfare workers, 30 artists and about 100 musicians and entertainers. Business establishments were mostly of the service type, particularly *cantinas*.[52]

Mexican Americans have shown sporadic interest in unions. They participated in large strikes of agricultural workers in southern California in 1928, 1930, 1933, and 1936.[53] The last strike in particular was broken up only

[51] Governor's Interracial Commission of Minnesota, *The Mexican in Minnesota* (St. Paul, Minnesota: State of Minnesota, 1948), p. 15.

[52] Frank X. Paz, *Mexican-Americans in Chicago* (Chicago: Chicago Council of Social Agencies, 1948).

[53] Carey McWilliams, *North from Mexico*, chap. x. He writes: "In midsummer 1936 a strike of 2500 Mexicans tied up for several weeks a $20,000,000 citrus crop in Orange County. During this strike Orange County was in a virtual state of siege. . . . Over 400 special armed guards were recruited. Two hundred arrested strikers were formally arraigned in

by the wholesale use of violence, seriously damaging if not destroying the myth that every Mexican was a docile peon. Other strikes during the thirties were in Arizona, Idaho, Washington, Colorado, Michigan, and Texas. The largest of these were the pecan-sheller strike in San Antonio in 1934 and the coal mine strike in Gallup, New Mexico, in 1934-35. In Chicago, Mexicans received unions with enthusiasm, which has gradually waned. Nevertheless, when as late as 1947 some Mexicans were imported as a group as strikebreakers in Chicago, they all joined the union when they discovered what the situation really was.

A group of Mexican laborers in southern California, none of whom were union members, were asked, "Do you like labor unions?" Their answers included: "Yes. Union workers get more money." "Sure, if I could be a union musician I would be rich and live like a king." "No. But I like the money they get us." "Yes, I guess I'd make more money. I don't like John L. Lewis, tho'." "No, if the unions aren't stopped pretty soon this won't be a free country any more." "No, you have to pay too much back to them—besides, they're crooked."

Unions are particularly important to a partially assimilated group like the Mexicans, for, depending on the composition and leadership of the local, unionization may have an important bearing on the rate of acculturation, the character of interaction between the Mexicans and other groups, and participation in civic, recreational, and political activities.[54]

Any generally poverty-stricken group can be expected to have a high percentage of social welfare clients. This

---

an outdoor . . . courtroom. Guards with rifles and shotguns patrolled the citrus belt. . . . I was in court one day when fifty or more strikers were brought in. . . . The Los Angeles *Examiner* spoke feelingly of the 'quieting effects of wholesale arrests.' "

[54] McWilliams, *North from Mexico*, p. 193.

is true of Mexican Americans, and was particularly true
during the depression.

> It cost the County of Los Angeles $77,249.29 to repatriate one
> trainload, but the saving in relief was estimated at $347,468.41
> for this one shipment. In 1932 alone over 11,000 Mexicans were
> repatriated from Los Angeles. . . . Of the 175,000 Mexicans who
> . . . met the agricultural labor requirements of the whole state . . .
> there were possibly not more than 10 per cent available in 1936.[55]

Despite these astonishing figures, Mexicans benefited less
than the general population both during the depression
and under the present Social Security Act. Many, during
the depression, were denied WPA work because they were
aliens. The present Social Security Act is of less than
normal benefit to them, for agricultural workers are specifically excluded from Old Age and Survivors Insurance,
Unemployment Insurance, and Industrial Accident Insurance. Old Age Assistance, and Aid to Dependent Children, Aid to the Blind, and the Rehabilitation Program
are usually closed to them too, because of the residence
requirements that an alien must have lived in the United
States for 25 years, and even a citizen must have lived in
the state in which he makes application for 5 of the last
9 years. It probably should be added that Mexicans frequently have the reputation of liking relief. This is at
least partially true, but it stems from the pitifully low
wages they receive when working, rather than any special
laziness or lack of moral fiber, as has been frequently
charged. A man whose children are better fed and clothed
by social welfare aid than they are when he is fully employed may be foolish to work.

The contribution of Mexican workers to United States
economic welfare can best be seen in the Southwestern
region. Beginning with a scant production in 1900, by
1929 this region was producing 40 per cent of the nation's

[55] *Ibid.*, pp. 185-86.

fruit and truck crops. Mexican labor constituted 65 per cent to 85 per cent of the common labor used in the production of these crops. From 1900 to 1940, Mexican labor constituted 60 per cent of the common labor in the mines of the Southwest, and from 60 per cent to 90 per cent of the section and extra gangs employed on 18 Western railroads. "Obviously the transformation of the Southwest which has occurred in the last forty years was largely made possible by the use of Mexican labor."[56]

As a generalization, industrial positions are more readily available to Mexican Americans the farther north they live, and the fewer their number in the population. Despite these advances, Mexican Americans with industrial jobs have remained marginal workers. A not inconsiderable number have been able to retain stable industrial work, and new fields have been opened at least part way for young Mexican Americans; but on the whole they, like other minority groups, were the first to lose their jobs when the postwar slackening of employment occurred in the swollen war industries. Only in part has the Mexican American been able to retain his wartime economic advances.

[56] *Ibid.*

III.

MAJOR MEXICAN-AMERICAN INSTITUTIONS

Educational Problems. Many of the social problems of Mexican Americans are youth problems; the most important of these are closely related to education. In San Antonio, in 1930, Mexicans made up 90 per cent of the city's illiterates; 15.7 per cent of the total Mexican population 10 years of age and over were illiterate; at least 1 in 3 Mexican children entering school dropped out before finishing the fifth grade. In Crystal City, Texas, in 1938, the average 18-year-old Mexican American had not completed the third grade.[1] Tuck's sampling of immigrant Mexicans in "Descanso" in 1944 showed 26 per cent illiteracy; a larger sampling which included Mexican Americans of all generations showed 4.3 per cent illiteracy, exactly the national average, and revealed no illiterates outside the immigrant generation.[2]

[1] Selden C. Menefee, *Mexican Migratory Workers of South Texas* (Washington: Government Printing Office, 1941), pp. xv, 47.
[2] Ruth D. Tuck, *Not with the Fist* (New York: Harcourt, Brace, and Co., 1946), p. 63.

Figures on illiteracy do not show the true problem of Mexican education, however, for it centers chiefly in the early dropping-out of scholastics rather than their failure ever to attend. It is estimated that 75 per cent of the Mexican children of school age are in school, and that the number in high school is only about ⅓ what it should be on the basis of population. Little[3] found in Texas in 1942-43 only 53 per cent of the children of school age of Mexican descent actually enrolled and attending regularly; 72 per cent of those enrolled were aged 6-12 inclusive; 68 per cent of the children 6-12 were in the first three grades, and 52 per cent of all Spanish-speaking scholastics were in the first three grades. Over 69 per cent of the Mexican Americans as compared with 25 per cent of the Anglo school children were below average for their grade. Great numbers of Spanish-speaking children are retarded from 1 to 11 years. The mean age of first graders was 9.6 for Mexican Americans and 7.9 for Anglos.[4] In Texas, despite a compulsory education law, minority-group children are not forced to attend school. The fact that state funds are distributed on the basis of scholastics, rather than on children regularly attending, is a significant factor, for money collected on nonattending Mexican children may be spent on the Anglo children who do attend.

Of the 699,220 Mexicans of foreign or mixed parentage, English was the mother tongue of only 7 per cent, the lowest percentage of any of the 19 mother tongues tabulated.[5] This may be accounted for by the recency of Mexican immigration and by the fact that most Mexican immigrants settled in predominantly Spanish-speaking

[3] Wilson Little, *Spanish-Speaking Children in Texas* (Austin, Texas: University of Texas Press, 1944), pp. 64-65.

[4] C. L. Yarbrough, "Age-Grade Status of Texas Children of Latin-American Descent," *Journal of Educational Research*, XL (Sept., 1946), 14-27.

[5] Sixteenth Census of the United States, *Population by Mother Tongue*, p. 6.

subcommunities where English is little needed. It is generally agreed that the chief problem of the Mexican children is their linguistic handicap. The normal procedure is to admit children at 6 or 7, carry on all the teaching in English, and trust that the child will learn the language and the content material simultaneously. This does occur under optimum conditions, i.e., when the child is bright, strongly motivated, sympathetically taught, and wholeheartedly included by his classmates in all activities. Unfortunately such a situation is rare, and most commonly the child learns both language and content imperfectly. The language handicap, difficult at any time, may become progressively worse until it becomes insurmountable and

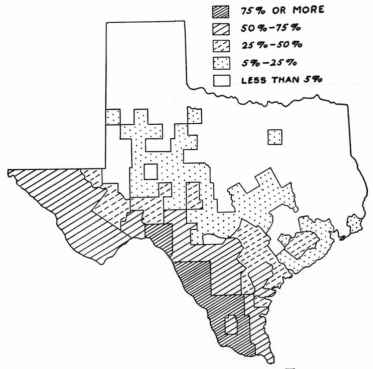

SPANISH-SPEAKING SCHOLASTICS IN TEXAS

the child fails repeatedly and finally leaves school. In addition to the "sink or swim" method described above there are several other methods which may be used for the instruction of the Spanish-speaking child. One is to admit the child at 5, use Spanish to teach English, and admit the child to regular work at age 6. Another method, successfully used in Puerto Rico, is to admit the child at 6, teach oral English and written Spanish for a year and a half, and then teach written English. This technique when used experimentally promised more than the others, but before it could be widely used in this country we would have to have more study, more and better texts and collateral materials, and specially trained teachers.

None of the above techniques is nearly so common as simply segregating the Mexican children until they learn English. Sometimes this means separate rooms, but in many areas it means separate school buildings. This segregation has arisen in different areas for different reasons. In areas where, 30 years ago, Mexican families were transported in wholesale and illegal fashion for cheap labor, were exploited and looked down upon as completely as were Negroes, segregation in the public schools has been the natural outgrowth of economic and social discrimination. In such cases "segregated" has meant "second-class," as it so commonly does in the South. In larger cities the location of Mexicans in separate subcommunities has meant that ordinary school districting has placed the majority of Spanish-speaking students in the same school. These schools may or may not be inferior to other schools. Still another type of segregation has been common; as a means of combating the language handicap of the Mexican children, they have been placed in separate rooms or schools until they could compete with English-speaking children. The argument is that if they have to compete in English with Anglos, they will fail repeatedly in the first few grades and drop out in discouragement. Hence, until they have mastered English they must not be expected to compete except within their own group.[6] This period is most commonly held to be the first three or four grades.[7] As a pedagogical device this technique has some merit, but it also has definite drawbacks. Evidence shows that when Spanish-speaking students are placed with English-speaking students and hear only English in the classroom and on the playground, their progress in the language is much faster. Moreover, when Mexican-American children are segregated until they reach high school, Anglo children have by then developed attitudes of superiority which cause the continuation and even intensification of discriminatory practices in high school and afterwards. Feelings of inferiority and rebellion engendered in Spanish-speaking children by such experiences in the school may lead to unhealthy attitudes in general and delinquency in particular.

The chief objection by the parents of students who attend segregated classes or schools is that the criterion for segregation is too often the parents' national origin rather than bilingualism. Some credence is lent this complaint by the number of cases on record of children of Mexican blood who, though their mother tongue is English, have been forced to attend segregated schools because of their alleged language handicap. Such problems eventually led to suits against a number of school boards until

[6] Burbank, California, has made use of a unique system whereby all Spanish-speaking students are kept together for three years in one nongraded class managed by two subject-matter teachers and one activity teacher. At any given time the activity teacher will have about half the class engaged in noncontent work. The others are divided into small groups and get much individual attention; workbooks and projects are used as adjuncts in rectifying the weaknesses of each student. At the end of three years the pupils are admitted to nonsegregated fourth grade classes.

[7] Little, Spanish-Speaking Children in Texas, pp. 64-66, found wide variations in Texas; segregation occurring not at all, in grades 1-2, 1-3, 1-4, 1-5, 1-6, 1-12, depending on the local situation.

in 1946 a federal court in California ruled that children can be segregated only if each child is given an intensive examination based on foreign language impediments regardless of his ethnic traits of ancestry. In this case briefs of *amicus curiae* were filed on behalf of the Mexicans by the National Lawyers Guild, the American Jewish Congress, the National Association for the Advancement of Colored People, the American Civil Liberties Union, the Japanese-American Citizens League and the attorney general of California. With such an array of legal talent in opposition it is no wonder that one school board's contention that Mexicans were inferior and unhygienic received scant consideration. The contention of another school board that Mexican children should be segregated in school because Mexicans depreciated housing values met a like fate.

In 1948 a federal court in Texas ruled that Mexican-American children could be segregated in the first grade only, and then only if they were unfamiliar with the English language. The most telling arguments in this case were that no attempt was made to segregate children whose mother tongue was German, Italian, Yiddish, Polish, or some other, and that special teaching techniques adapted to bilingual students were rarely if ever used. It was shown that segregation was chiefly the result of the belief of certain teachers, parents, and school boards that Mexican-American children were usually dirty, immoral, spreaders of germs, stupid, lazy, or otherwise generally undesirable. As a result of the Texas and California court decisions, segregation has markedly declined except as it is the product of school district gerrymandering which makes some schools predominantly Mexican because of the residential area they serve. Aside from these court decisions there has always existed the likelihood of some mixing in one or more schools of a locality, even though there might be a regular "Mexican" school. While officially the ability to speak English has been the criterion for entering a mixed school, actually the class status of the parents, their aggressiveness and prosperity, the cleanliness and mannerliness of the children, and the quota of Spanish-speaking children already in the school have been basic determining factors.

Dallas Johnson[8] reports a community in California in which Mexican children had attended segregated schools for thirty years when a new superintendent tried to merge the schools. His opportunity came when it became necessary to build fences around the schools to protect them from vandalism. He pointed out to the school board that merging the schools would make an immediate saving of $5,000 and a later saving in cost of maintenance and of staff while at the same time giving a better education to all children. In spite of pressure by townspeople the merger took place, enrollment increased, and soon it was possible to divide each grade into a fast and slow section. Contrary to the expectation of some Anglos, for Anglos and Mexicans in each section the rates of progress and the percentages of high achievement and failure were about equal.

The segregation of Mexican-American children and their linguistic difficulties are simply two of their significant educational problems. Equally significant, but by no means equally dramatic, is their in general relatively low economic, social, and cultural level. These factors would be serious handicaps for any children, and the superimposition of segregation, bilingualism, and cultural difficulties often results in these children's not being accepted as real partners in democratic living by the majority group—many even develop characteristics which make for further cleavage. Occupational training and health education are

[8] Dallas Johnson, "The Fenced Tolerance In," *Survey Graphic*, XXXVI (July, 1947), 398-99.

problem areas frequently found, and some of the more alert school systems report that they have considerable difficulty in presenting the Mexican cultural heritage adequately to either the minority or majority group. Certainly an indispensable element in a complete school program for mixed schools must be education of Anglo children in the values of the Mexican culture: to teach a smattering of the language, some songs, and an appreciation of Mexican paintings, dances, recreation, food, customs, holidays, and history—all those things which will break down strangeness and the incomprehensibility of different ways of living.

Only in recent years have teachers' colleges become very actively aware that the successful instruction of Spanish-speaking children requires special teaching methods and classroom materials, plus some knowledge and understanding of the Mexican-American child's social characteristics, economic background, cultural heritage, and language. Texas, New Mexico, Arizona, and California recently have published teachers' guides to teaching Spanish-speaking children in the primary grades.

Added to all these problems, some children must move about with their migratory parents engaged in agricultural labor. This means shifting schools at best, and at worst attending school for only a small portion of the year or not at all. Menefee[9] found among migratory laborers that about 1 in 6 children aged 7-10 and about 2 in 5 of those 11-13 years of age attended school the full year; 14-year-olds had completed, on the average, three years of school work; 1 in 5 had never completed the first grade and only 1 in 7 had completed five or more years of school. Several plans have attempted to cope with this problem, none very satisfactorily. California has a few trailer schools which follow the migrant children, but these

[9] Menefee, *Mexican Migratory Workers*, pp. 44-45.

are inadequate in many ways. Special funds are available for school districts where migrant children swell the load unduly during part of the year. Some schools start at 7 A.M. and stop at noon so that the children may work half a dav in the fields. None of these plans has been particularly successful, a fact which is not surprising since a school for migrant children may have a pupil turnover averaging 20 per cent a month.

In view of all these factors one can expect relatively few Mexican-American students to go through high school and college. In one San Antonio "Mexican" school, of 192 students graduating only 5 went to college. A higher proportion of girls than boys finish high school, probably because girls may then find some employment as office workers while boys find the same limited economic opportunities with or without a high-school education. A study of 33 colleges and universities in Texas in 1945-46 showed that Spanish-name students formed 1.6 per cent of the total enrollment although they made up 20.4 per cent of the white population of school age: 6 schools reported workshops and courses centered on the education of Mexican Americans; 4 reported courses specially designed for Spanish-speaking students; 5 reported some type of counseling program or advisory staff for Spanish-speaking students; in 11 schools, Mexican Americans and Anglo students are encouraged to live together; 9 reported scholarships offered especially to Spanish-speaking students.[10]

Despite this situation in the past, the educational picture for Mexican-American children is a constantly brightening one. Segregation is both less common and less vicious. School systems and individual teachers are better equipped and more deeply motivated to handle special problems. Mexican-American standards of living have

[10] Ruth Ann Fogartie, *Texas-Born Spanish-Name Students in Texas Colleges and Universities (1945-46)* (Austin, Texas: University of Texas Press, Inter-American Education Occasional Papers, III, 1948).

improved. An increasing percentage of the children are children of native-born parents, and bring to school a considerable, if imperfect, knowledge of American customs and language. In short, at the chief points of tension the strain is gradually lessening, and at the same time better techniques for dealing with such problems are being developed and more widely used. Each year a greater number of Mexican-American youth are finishing high school, and, particularly under the G. I. Bill, more are attending college.

Religion. In Mexico the vast majority of the population is Catholic. The Mexican church is a mixture of paganism and Catholicism with much emphasis on local saints, supernatural occurrences, and emotional experiences. Transplanted to the United States, the Mexican Catholic church loses many of these emphases and loses some of its fervor; churchgoing becomes more nominal. Most Mexican Americans remain nominally Catholic; they are baptized, married, and buried with Catholic rites. However, the number of individuals who regularly attend church is not large, and this group is made up chiefly of older women, old men, and young children still under a mother's guidance. Males in general and adolescents and young adults of both sexes are likely to be indifferent, yet few will ever relinquish this token bond with the Church, and do sometimes attend.[11] There are seventeen "Mexican" Catholic churches in Los Angeles, for example.

The influence of the Church on the Mexican immigrant and his family is extremely variable. Probably the most common complaints against priests are that they are too conservative and are interested only in the religious aspects of the life of their parishioners. While this is true in some localities, it is completely untrue elsewhere.[12] Some

[11] Tuck, *Not with the Fist*, pp. 152-53
[12] A priest in Austin, Texas, worked for eight years before finally getting a program accepted for bringing groups of rural Mexican-American girls

churches have virtually no "extra" church organizations, but in others such organizations are varied and potent. By all means the most influential—or at least the most popular—of these is the Catholic Youth Organization. Oftentimes the CYO offers the only organized recreational outlet for adolescent boys in the *colonia*, the Mexican-American section of town.[13] The formal influence of the Catholic church appears difficult to predict in that sometimes it seems to have no overt influence on people's attitudes and actions. Suddenly, however, the full force of its weight will overwhelmingly sway what had been evenly divided opinion.

Segregation typically exists in the Southwest in both Catholic and Protestant churches. It is decried in principle by both groups, but churches are usually near the people they serve, and since Mexican Americans live in segregated communities—as the result of both active and passive segregation—there are "Mexican" and "Anglo" churches. This differentiation is heightened by the fact that many of the older people speak English very poorly, so that sermons, responses, hymns, and other parts of the service must be in Spanish. Consequently the clergy probably will have to be Spanish-speaking. Such segregation is rarely absolute; i.e., certain Mexicans or occasional Mexican visitors may be accepted or even welcomed in Anglo churches in the Southwest, and vice versa, but real integration is rare within the region. Upper-class Mexican Americans are of course much more acceptable than lower-class ones, and since the average Mexican American is in the

---

from the country to Austin for a week. He believes many of them will come to the city eventually, and should know about the city even if they do not. He shows them the sights, explains all about city life, city customs, and city pitfalls. He was delayed in getting the program really under way because of the reluctance of parents to permit the girls to be outside the home for a week, even under the care of a priest.

[13] Cf. Griffith, *American Me* (Boston: Houghton-Mifflin Co., 1948), pp. 186-90.

lowest socioeconomic class, he is not welcome for another reason. Only in the small towns where there is but one church of a kind is any real integration likely in the Southwest. Outside the areas of large Mexican-American population, integration is the rule rather than the exception. Protestant churches have made considerably larger numbers of converts among Mexican Americans in the United States than among residents in Mexico; the percentage, although small, is probably five times as great as in Mexico. The three major reasons for this change in religious allegiance seem to be: (1) active proselyting by various Protestant churches; (2) social welfare services, settlement houses, recreation programs and other extra-ecclesiastical activities of Protestant groups; (3) the general assimilative process at work on second- and third-generation young people. That the number changing to Protestantism is not greater is probably due to weaknesses on the part of some churches; Mexican Protestant churches are usually of the mission type, small, and rarely self-supporting; frequently they do a poor public relations job, do not make full use of musical possibilities, and seriously lack physical attractiveness.[14] Protestant settlement houses do not make a wide impression, but they fill an important place in the growth of many Mexican-American leaders whom they help with encouragement, imparting American outlook and industry and providing scholarships.

Those who do become Protestants are under continual fire from priests and good Catholics. They show some tendency to be narrow in their moral outlook[15] and to attach themselves to sects of the Pentecostal type; others enter the Baptist, Congregational, Lutheran, Methodist or Presbyterian denominations. Protestants tend to be in the

[14] *Ibid.*, pp. 190-95.
[15] Part of the congregation of one church, for example, objected vocally to the new pastor and his family going to picture shows, smoking in the home, and reading frivolous books.

middle rather than at either extreme of the Mexican-American socioeconomic scale. Broom and Shevsky state that the church, Catholic or Protestant, is the principal agency of cultural conservatism for Mexicans in the United States and reinforces the separateness of the group. They feel that competition between the church and the mission reveals and accentuates cleavages in the Mexican population and is an obstacle to concensus.[16]

The Mexican-American Family. The majority of family heads in this group have come from a comparatively simple economy and culture in which custom and tradition dominate, and in which family life is somewhat controlled by community opinion. Family authority is usually vested in the principal wage-earner or the person in control of the family finances, who is usually the father or eldest male. Other family members are somewhat under his control, and this relationship may extend to grown children who have established their own homes. Godparents are usually chosen for the children, are responsible for their baptism, and often are loved and respected second only to the parents.[17]

Although outward signs of affection may not be common, family ties are usually strong, and divorce and desertion are more rare than among Anglo families. In Texas, in a town in the Winter Garden area,[18] the median family included 5.5 persons. More than 80 per cent of all families were of the "normal" type: husband and wife, with or without children. San Antonio Mexican families averaged 4.6 persons, but only 57 per cent were the "normal" type, and 31 per cent were broken families; 12 per

---

[16] Leonard Broom and Eshref Shevsky, "Mexicans in the United States: A Problem in Social Differentiation," *Sociology and Social Research,* XXXVI (Jan.-Feb., 1952), 150-58.

[17] Cf. Robert C. Jones, "Ethnic Family Patterns: The Mexican Family in the United States," *American Journal of Sociology,* LIII (May, 1948), 450-52.

[18] Menefee, *Mexican Migratory Workers,* p. 11.

cent were single-person families. The extended-family system exists very widely in the first generation. This type of family grouping is defended as giving a feeling of security and being "nice for the children." To this extended family-circle the second generation adds friendships formed Anglo style in the school, the church, or the neighborhood. Although these new relationships tend to lessen interest in the larger family group, the almost complete lack of woman's clubs and organizations prevents a very close approximation of the Anglo pattern. Even where second- or third-generation families have acquired such Anglo patterns as the egalitarian family and the limiting of family size, the large-family feeling, the designation of godparents, strictness with girls, and considerable intrafamily visiting continue to play a significant role. The attitude that the happiness and welfare of the individual should be somewhat subordinated to that of the family has not disappeared. For example, the interest of the family is more closely followed in courtship and marriage than in the Anglo culture. The old-country patterns of the bridegroom's asking the father for the bride's hand, and of the bridegroom's paying for the wedding celebration have not died out but are definitely declining. Considering what Mexican-American family income usually is, weddings are likely to be extremely expensive. Early marriage and parents 18 or 19 years old are considerably more common than among Anglos. Where job opportunities are strictly limited, the Mexican-American male may be making as much money at 18 as he will at any other time in his life.

As in Mexico, the mother is the chief religious influence in the home. The girls' religious upbringing is given some care, but the father and older boys generally show only a desultory interest. So, too, the mother is the chief inculcator of morals for the girls and younger boys, the father attempting that role for the older boys, again with possibly desultory interest only. In some families, of course, the father is the actual as well as the titular preceptor, guardian, and guide.

Under the impact of immigration, migration, cultural conflict, urban living, and minority-group status, many old culture traits normally decline. Those assumed to be of most value to the individual and the group are those preserved longest, so marriage and family life have been relatively slow to change. Yet even in this important area the web of culture is being rather badly broken and no longer exists as a completely integrated system. The dominant role of the father has tended to decline. The wife may remain subordinate, but the sons are more emancipated and not infrequently the eldest son supersedes the father as mentor and protector for the younger children because he knows more about the American culture. The older girls, particularly if employed, are much less subordinate than the mother, and may refuse a completely subordinate role when they become wives. If the father, as is not uncommon, suffers long periods of unemployment, his status suffers correspondingly. First-generation men generally expect their wives and children to behave according to the pattern in Mexico and oppose the Americanizing of wife or home. They are less likely, however, to oppose the Americanization of their children, especially the boys.[19]

Because of their poor economic circumstances, most members of the Mexican minority are forced to live in slums or slumlike areas of low rentals; they are frequently compelled to keep roomers. The persons to whom rooms are rented often are relatives, but they may be strangers to whom space is rented for purely economic reasons. The presence of outsiders in an overcrowded, dilapidated, un-

[19] Norman D. Humphrey, "The Changing Structure of the Detroit Mexican Family: An Index of Acculturation," *American Sociological Review*, IX (Dec., 1944), 622-26.

sanitary home is known to have a deteriorating effect upon family life. Patterns of sexual behavior are subject to the additionally disorganizing and demoralizing influences which exist in any slum.

Wherever there are considerable numbers of any minority group, intermarriage with the majority group or with other minority groups is likely to occur. This is true of the Mexican-American minority, but there are very few satisfactory statistics on such phenomena. When the minority group has a lower status, its females are more likely to intermarry than in the case of a minority group with a very low proportion of women. No great amount of intermarriage, however, does occur. In Minnesota a 1946 study[20] of the St. Paul Mexican colony revealed only 33 cases of intermarriage out of some 750 families. Three of these were with Indians, 6 with Negroes, and 20 with Anglos of various nationalities. In most Northern cities intermarriage is commonest with whatever immigrant group is nearest the Mexican community. In Chicago, for example, this is the Italian group.

A recent study of intermarriage on the West Coast[21] showed that in a group of 1,000 consecutive marriages, about 3.5 per cent were between Anglos and Mexican Americans, the marriages of Anglo males to Mexican-American females making up about 80 per cent of this total. A concurrent sample of much greater proportions which did not record Anglo-Mexican-American marriages showed that other intermarriages ranked in the following order: (1) Filipino male-Mexican female; (2) Negro male-Mexican female; (3) Mexican male-Filipino female; (4) Chinese male-Mexican female; (5) Japanese male-Mexican female; (6) Mexican male-Negro female;

[20] Governor's Interracial Commission of Minnesota, *Mexicans in Minnesota* (St. Paul, Minnesota: State of Minnesota, 1948), pp. 31-32.

[21] John H. Burma, "Research Note on the Measurement of Interracial Marriage," *American Journal of Sociology*, LVI (May, 1952), 587-89.

(7) Mexican male-Japanese female; and (8) Mexican male-Chinese female. Mexican men who married Anglo women tended to be younger than those who married Mexican women. Mexican women who married non-Mexicans tended to be overrepresented in the 15-19-year and 30-44-year age groups, and underrepresented in the rest, as compared with those who married Mexican men.

Apart from the study reported above, there is some evidence that intermarriage is somewhat more common within the upper and lower classes than within the middle class. Intermarriage between an Anglo and an upper-class Mexican American seems the most acceptable to Anglos, probably because in this class color and culture differences are likely to be less. If assimilation continues, and if there is no continuing large emigration from Mexico, it may be expected that intermarriage will gradually increase and will continue to be greater numerically than the intermarriage of Anglos with other minority groups.

Housing. Always in the Southwest and commonly throughout the rest of the United States, the Mexican lives in a segregated section of town. He calls it the *barrio* or the *colonia;* Anglos call it "Mextown," "Spiktown," "Little Mexico," or some such term. By whatever name it is known, it can be recognized as a distinct and substandard area; its reputation, among the Anglos, is not a very savory one. Probably three-fourths of all Mexicans live in such *colonias,* varying in size from a cluster of shacks to communities of several thousand. Wherever located, the *colonia* is likely to be "on the other side of" something. It is a satellite community, separated from the parent community by psychic and social isolation, with definite if unverbalized barriers between it and the parent community. The segregation is not wholly active, but it is none the less real and confining, and recognized by both groups; it may lead

Anglos to charge that Mexicans are clannish, unfriendly, and withdrawn—quite incorrectly.[22]

The business places of the *colonia* are relatively numerous, small, and of the "family store" type; although usually owned by the Mexicans themselves, a few are Jewish clothing stores or Chinese groceries. There is a high ratio of taverns, and probably a Spanish-language movie or two. Just as in an Anglo community, the poorest houses are likely to be nearest the business section, with housing improving as one moves outward. Streets are less likely to be paved than in the Anglo sections, and alleys may serve the normal functions of streets. In a Northern city the *colonia* is more like any other foreign settlement; its boundaries are less sharply defined, and its people more likely to be looked upon as a nationality rather than a racial group. In the North, segregation is almost entirely voluntary; in many areas of the Southwest and West it is involuntary, sometimes because of restrictive covenants, more often because of an informal unwillingness to rent or sell to Mexicans.

Gamio[23] lists four types of housing typically found in the *colonia*. The best is the small, modern house, like that of middle-class or lower middle-class Anglos. The most unusual is the one-story, crib type of tenement, much like the *vecindad* in Old Mexico, with common walls and with fronts on a street or on a court. These vary considerably in quality, but usually there are only one or two rooms per family. The third type, and probably the most common, is the small two- or three-room house, built like the houses of lower-class Anglos and typically in a state of partial disrepair. Almost as common is the fourth type, the hovel of wood, tin, thatch, canvas, packing boxes or any combination thereof, with two to four shacks to a lot.

[22] McWilliams, *North from Mexico*, pp. 217-20.
[23] Gamio, *Mexican Immigration*, p. 146.

In 1938, about two-thirds of San Antonio's 100,000 Mexican and Mexican-American population lived in four square miles on the West Side—one of the most extensive slums to be found in any American city. Menefee's study of the pecan shellers in this section[24] showed that the median home housed over 2 persons per room; about 1 in 20 had 5 or more persons per room. Only 25 per cent of these homes had electric lights, 12 per cent had running water inside, 9 per cent had inside toilets; in all, over 90 per cent were substandard. Comparable situations exist in Denver, Los Angeles, and other cities with a high proportion of Mexicans. With the coming of government slum clearance projects, some very definite if spotty improvement has occurred. San Antonio has a long-range housing program already under way; Mexicans have benefited in Denver, El Paso, Austin, and other cities, and occupy 20 per cent of the public housing in Los Angeles.

Bad though the situation is in the large cities, it may be even worse in the smaller cities and towns. Hazard[25] estimated that of the 70,000 workers, mostly Mexicans, who worked in beets and potatoes in Colorado, Wyoming, and Montana, 60,000 lived in houses that had no sanitary sewage disposal, 67,000 had no garbage disposal, 33,000 had no bathing facilities, 34,000 had a questionable water supply, and an additional 10,000 had only ditchwater for drinking. The average house had two and a half rooms for an average family of 5. A study of the so-called permanent homes of Mexican agricultural workers living in South Texas[26] indicated that the houses were mostly unpainted one- or two-room frame shacks with single walls, the cracks being covered on the outside by narrow wooden

[24] Menefee, *Mexican Migratory Workers*, pp. 43-46. See also Max Handman, "San Antonio," *Survey*, LXVI (May 1, 1931), 163-66.
[25] C. E. Hazard, *Welfare of Families of Sugar Beet Laborers*, (Children's Bureau Publication Number 247 [Washington: United States Department of Labor, 1939]).
[26] Menefee, *Mexican Migratory Workers*, pp. 41-42.

strips. Tin roofs predominated, as did dirt floors, and most of the houses had at least two glass windows. The poorer houses were patched together with scrap lumber, old signboards, tar paper, tin, and adobe. Less than 10 per cent had electric lights and still fewer indoor plumbing; the usual procedure was for several families to share a single outdoor water faucet. A few did not even have stoves; they cooked outdoors when possible and in open washtubs inside when necessary. Five per cent of the families had 10 or more persons living in one- or two-room houses. More than 50 per cent owned their own shacks, but most of these rented the land on which the shacks stood. This kind of arrangement is one of the most vicious problems of lower-class housing for Mexicans; the land rent is usually very cheap, but there is no incentive for the renter to make improvements on the shack he has built, for he will not be able to take it with him if he goes, and he is subject to eviction like any other renter. Hence such shacks continually get worse, incredible as that may seem.

The H—— Camp is a good illustration of the poorest type of slum.[27] In Los Angeles County, California, in a town of 30,000 it is one of 8 camps. It is 3 blocks long and 5 blocks wide, containing 168 houses and nearly 1,000 persons. It is on the bank of the Rio Hondo, and the drainage is so poor that the camp stands in water throughout the rainy season. A nicely graded street runs to within a few blocks of the camp but only two deeply rutted, dirt streets lead into the settlement. There are no trees in the *colonia* to relieve the unpainted, weatherbeaten shacks built by the owners, in the majority of cases with refuse lumber from the railroad. Sometimes a lean-to or dilapidated auto shed has been built on; sometimes there is a

[27] From an unpublished manuscript by Sue Starr, Pomona College, Pomona, California, 1947.

chicken pen, and always a privy, for there are no indoor plumbing facilities in the camp. There are frequent attempts to beautify the porches and front yards with flowers or potted plants, but for the most part the backyards are littered with rubbish. Heat is furnished by the kitchen stove; the laundry is done outdoors over a fire and the dirty water is dumped in the yard. Some of the houses have electric lights, but there is not one refrigerator and only one bathtub in the camp.

It must not be inferred that this sort of housing situation is satisfactory to most Mexicans; they are often very bitter, and, far from being resigned to it, they plan and save for the day when they can "move the children to a decent house." Unsuccessful efforts to beautify the shacks are everywhere apparent, but a few geraniums in tin cans and colored pictures on the walls cannot counteract the effects of stark poverty. Second-generation Mexican Americans in particular are unwilling to remain in such surroundings, and strive to move to better areas. A few own their own house and lot, and where such is the case their interest in improving their property commonly surpasses that of their Anglo neighbors.

Health. The rural and urban housing and living conditions of many Mexicans is a serious health menace. Lack of money, ignorance of sanitation, lack of doctors and trained midwives, and reliance on herbal medication all combine to put the Mexicans in one of the most serious health situations in the United States. Everywhere the infant mortality rate, the tuberculosis rate, and the malaria, dysentery, and typhoid rates of the Mexicans are much above the average. In San Antonio the Mexicans, making up 38 per cent of the population, had 72 per cent of the deaths from tuberculosis. The infant mortality rate, one of our most delicate indices of general social well-being, was 120 per 1,000, about three times the national average.[28]

[28] Selden C. Menefee and Orin C. Cassmore, *The Pecan Shellers of San Antonio* (Washington: Government Printing Office, 1940), pp. 46-47.

The chief cause of infant death in San Antonio in 1944 was diarrhea, resulting from the heavy growth of bacteria from such unsanitary conditions as open sewage; of the 274 children who died of diarrhea that year, 97 per cent were Mexican Americans.[29]

A study of the families of agricultural workers in a South Texas county showed that beans, rice, potatoes, and tortillas were the staple diet; vegetables and fruits were infrequently eaten by many families even though easily and cheaply available. After infancy milk was rarely used; only about 20 per cent of the children had as much as a pint of milk a day. Ninety per cent of the children under two years of age were still being breast-fed; just over 50 per cent of this group were receiving supplementary feedings of milk, and 18 per cent of these small children had supplementary milk only in their coffee. In only 18 per cent of the cases had the mothers consulted a physician concerning the baby's feeding. Among the younger children diarrhea was a significant cause of ill-health and an important cause of the infant mortality of 150 per 1,000, over three times the national average.

In about 40 per cent of the cases clinically studied, the children had positive tuberculin tests, showing that at some time they had been infected with tuberculosis. Over 25 per cent of the children studied were judged to need immediate medical care, while about 40 per cent were in good physical condition.[30]

Griffith[31] reports the same situation in California. In Los Angeles the rate of deaths per 100,000 from tuberculosis in 1930 was 73.8 for Anglos and 326.4 for Mexicans; by 1944 much improvement had occurred, but the rate

[29] Kibbe, Pauline R., *Latin Americans in Texas* (Albuquerque, N. M.: University of New Mexico Press, 1946), p. 132.

[30] Amber A. Warburton, Helen Wood, and Marian M. Crane, *The Work and Welfare of Agricultural Laborers in Hidalgo County, Texas* (Children's Bureau Publication 298 [Washington: United States Department of Labor, 1943]), pp. 55-56.

[31] Griffith, *American Me*, pp. 132-34.

was still nearly double for Mexicans—45 to 84. Even greater improvement has occurred in the infant mortality rate. In 1923 the rate per 100,000 for Anglos was 80.5 and for Mexicans 250.6; by 1944 it was 32.3 and 36.2, a comparatively insignificant difference. For children in Los Angeles under two years of age, respiratory diseases (principally pneumonia) were the chief cause of death, with gastroenteritis and malnutrition second and third— the latter setting the stage for much later ill-health. While the common use of home remedies, often superstitious in nature, adds to the bad effects of ill-health, second- and third-generation Mexicans are well aware of the problem, want health programs, advice, and clinics, and co-operate very well whenever these are available.

Classes. In Mexico, historically, there has been a virtual closed-class system. Over the years this relatively closed class-system has been modified and is now being liberalized even more. Despite this fact, most Mexican immigrants to this country, particularly upper-class ones, are observably more class-conscious than the average Anglo. Thus the organization and composition of any class system within the Mexican and Mexican-American group is of real social importance.

To the average Anglo there are two classes, lower and middle, in "Mextown." To the Mexican there are three. The lower class is the same in both classifications: poverty-stricken, dwelling in hovels, following the harvest or doing manual day labor, semi-illiterate, with little hope for the future, this group is at the bottom of the socioeconomic ladder. Above it, and observably so, are those whom the Anglo groups all together as middle class, and whom the Mexican divides into his middle and upper classes. At the bottom of this second continuum are the railroad workers and the semiskilled industrial workers; higher are the skilled workers, industrial artisans, and the smaller busi-

nessmen. They may be descendants of impoverished land-
owners, Mexicans who were of the middle class in Mexico
and retained their status when they migrated, or American-
born citizens who have worked up from the lower class.
Whatever their origin, most of these people own their own
homes, are respectable, literate citizens, and send their
children to public schools, sometimes to college. Where
there is a large Mexican community an upper class also
exists, made up chiefly of professional men and particularly
successful businessmen.[32] Both this group and the middle
class are smaller in numbers than would be expected, for
many persons of these classes have moved away from the
ethnic enclave and have tended to lose their identity with
it as they became more and more assimilated.

Occupation goes a long way in determining status. The
semiskilled or unskilled worker may be known as a "good
man," but he is seldom a "big man"; the ordinary agricultural or domestic worker never is. In addition to reaching the right occupation and its consequent financial return,
to achieve high status the Mexican or Mexican American
must be willing to serve the group. "A man must never
disclaim *la raza* . . . and must work for the betterment of
his group. . . . He must 'take an interest.'" The top
men are able to work in a wider, bolder fashion for *la raza*.
Education is also vital; "If pride in being Mexican is indispensable for status, education . . . comes second."[33]

The Anglo frequently misapplies some of his own
standards in assigning class status to a Mexican. He fails
to recognize, in the first place, how important it is to a
class-conscious, middle- or upper-class Mexican that he
not be grouped with all the rest. Secondly, many Anglos
assign status to a Mexican at least partly in terms of the
lightness of his skin. Actually there is little preoccupation

[32] Cf. Francis J. Brown and Joseph S. Roucek, *One America* (New
York: Prentice-Hall, 1945), pp. 497-509.
[33] Tuck, *Not with the Fists*, pp. 134-37.

with skin color among Mexicans. Sometimes there appears to be, because many Mexicans look down upon *indios* (Mexican Indians) as being of the lower class, and most of the *indios* are rather dark. Their lower status comes, however, not from color but from the sort of factors which bring lower-class status to any person, and which happen to be particularly common among this Indian group. A third error made by Anglos is to refer to upper-class, lighter Mexicans as Spanish. Although a few Mexican Americans selfishly foster the idea that there is a marked difference between the early Spanish settlers and the present *mestizos* (mixed Caucasian and Indian), the truth is that most of the old families in the beginning were *mestizos* too. As Tuck says, "They were pioneers, with all that implies, but . . . there is a cultural and genetic continuity between them and the late comer from Mexico."[34] Moreover, in Mexico, the middle and lower classes have no love for the Spaniard; middle-class Mexicans as a whole are proud of Mexico and have no more desire to be termed Spanish than a tenth-generation Yankee would care to be termed British. Nevertheless, particularly in southern California, there is a tendency to refer to favorable aspects of Mexican culture as Spanish. Advertisements in the Southwest often mention "Spanish" food, rarely "Mexican." As Mexican-American students enter college it is often tacitly assumed that they will refer to themselves and be referred to as Spanish. The role-playing involved has a tendency to make it appear that intellectual superiority and Spanish ancestry are definitely related.[35]

Usually leadership rests in the hands of various types of individuals from the middle and upper classes. Scher-

---

[34] *Ibid.*, p. 19.
[35] Edward C. McDonogh, "Status Levels of Mexicans," *Sociology and Social Research*, XXXV (Nov.-Dec., 1950), 450.

merhorn[36] lists five types of such leaders: (1) the natural leader, who is likely to have personal magnetism and the knack of getting his colleagues to follow him, but who lacks status in the Anglo community and is often of but limited vision; (2) the accommodating leader, who is friendly with the Anglos, derives much of his in-group status from this friendliness, and who is likely to be the Mexican counterpart of the Negro leader of the "Uncle Tom" type; (3) Mexican consuls, who may appear to be a present help in times of trouble for the alien, but who retard assimilation by encouraging the nostalgic nativism of *Mexicanismo*; (4) temporary political leaders, who achieve temporary status because they can get out a substantial vote by reason of their own enthusiasm and their acceptance in the neighborhood; (5) professional and businessman leaders, who have money, education, and the respect of the Anglos, but who may be somewhat isolated from the mass despite having status with them.

Whatever their other differences, all leaders must have one characteristic in common to be successful; they must have the welfare of *la raza* at heart, must not be ashamed of their people, and must really try to help them. Most leaders, moreover, are acculturated to American ways; they have Anglo friends and follow Anglo customs; they are the liaison and the spearhead. Yet they express the wish to combine the best in both ways of life, and demonstrate this wish by the continued incorporation in their lives of many Mexican culture traits.[37]

The Mexican community is still particularly dependent upon its leaders; energy and force still flow largely from the top down. In this state of affairs it is unfortunate that open fights for prestige among the leaders are not rare, fights usually due to pride, the conflict of personalities, or

[36] R. A. Schermerhorn, *These Our People* (Boston: D. C. Heath, 1949), pp. 195-96.
[37] Tuck, *Not with the Fist*, p. 138.

mutual suspicion of opportunism and exploitation, so that it is somewhat unusual for all the leaders in a fair-sized community to be working together at any one time. Mexican communities are like Anglo communities not only in this respect but also in that interclass unity is by no means universal or even particularly common. Also, especially in the North, the more settled immigrants put considerable social distance between themselves and the newcomers, as has been traditional in Anglo communities. Actually there is considerable vertical mobility in the Mexican community; the classes brought from Mexico are disappearing and new ones are taking their places. Now, some young, upper-class Mexican Americans had lower-class parents; and that, too, is in the American tradition.

Press. Like all large, recently arrived, foreign-language groups, the Mexican Americans have a special press, almost entirely in the language of the mother country. There are some 10 dailies with a circulation of about 72,000, 60 semiweeklies and weeklies with a circulation of about 85,000, and over 70 other papers of various sorts with a circulation of about 100,000. The largest of these, by far, is *La Prensa,* a weekly published in New York and also in several regional editions.[38] Like other foreign-language presses, this one appeals to people who either do not read English or who prefer to read Spanish. Moreover, there is among the Mexicans, as among other minorities, a very considerable group consciousness, and these special papers cover news of interest to the minority group which is unavailable or briefly treated in other papers. The Spanish-language press usually also includes more news of Mexico, as well as translations from the major news services. Otherwise the Mexican press, in Spanish or English, is very much like any general American newspaper with comics, sports page, society news, and so on, but

[38] *Interpreter Releases,* XX, No. 37, Series C, October 13, 1943, p. 297.

with a rather heavy emphasis on editorials and commen-
taries. It does not attempt to carry all news of all kinds,
and hence is a supplemental paper.

Especially when published in Spanish, the Mexican
newspaper has the problem of interesting two rather in-
compatible elements, the old people with their interest in
Mexico and their own age-group's activities, and the
younger group who have no special interest in Mexico and
who are interested in the activities of their age-group.
The papers serving the latter group are or soon will be
printed in English. Sometimes the editor, regardless of
the language of the paper, is something of a crusader, in
which case one of the purposes of the paper is to stimulate
minority morale and to protest discrimination. The Spanish-language press is on the decline and the English-language press for Mexicans is on the increase; it is probable
that in 15 years the Spanish-language press will virtually
have died out.

IV.

SOME CURRENT PROBLEMS OF MEXICAN AMERICANS

Organizations. In his own country the rural, lower middle-class Mexican does not readily form co-operative or social organizations. In this respect the immigrant in the United States changes rapidly and radically. For example, the Coordinating Council of Latin-American Youth in Los Angeles has had as many as 72 Mexican organizations represented at one time. Almost every type of organization is represented in the large Mexican community: religious, mutual aid, cultural, social, literary, recreational, and fraternal. Most originally were both mutual aid and recreational in theory, but the vast majority of local organizations have been in actuality social clubs of one kind or another. These local clubs sponsor dances, suppers, and other entertainments, but have no goal other than recreation. Many used to be supported by small monthly dues and paid small sick benefits. Such material benefit societies (*mutualistas*) were of considerable early significance, but, as has been true of other such immigrant groups, they proved to belong primarily to a transitional phase, and today do not appear to have any important place.

The largest of the nonlocal, serious organizations is the League of United Latin-American Citizens, the LULACS. It was born after World War I as a local organization in New Mexico, but was organized in 1929 in South Texas (where it is still strongest) as an interstate organization, and thereupon spread throughout the Southwest. Its membership is open only to citizens of Latin extraction, and it was the first major attempt of Mexican Americans to organize for the purpose of giving voice to their aspirations and needs as United States citizens. Its purposes are to encourage citizenship for alien Mexican immigrants; "to develop within the members of our race the best, purest, and most perfect type of true and loyal citizen of the United States of America," and at the same time "to maintain a sincere and respectful reverence for our racial origin of which we are proud"; to urge the necessity of learning and using English (the official language of the organization); to remove stigma and prejudice and racial, religious, and social discrimination; to foster education, culture, and tolerance, and to fight peonage, child labor and general mistreatment; to oppose radicalism and violence, but to seek equal representation on juries, in public office, in business, and in education, and to secure equal rights and opportunities. In order to disseminate information on these topics, the organization publishes, in English, the *LULAC News*.[1] Made up primarily of upper- and upper middle-class persons, the LULACS are sometimes accused of extreme conservatism. They make no pretext, however, of being a fighting organization, and the fact that they have formed many Ladies Councils indicates

[1] O. D. Weeks, "The Texas-Mexican and the Politics of South Texas," *American Political Science Review*, XXIV (Aug., 1930), 606-27.

to what an extent they have been willing to break with
Mexican tradition.

The oldest of the large organizations is the Spanish-
American Alliance (*La Alianza Hispano-Americano*). It
is a fraternal and benefit secret society with some 275
lodges throughout the Southwest, encompassing both
Mexicans and Spanish Americans. Each lodge is largely
independent, but low-cost life insurance and burial benefits, and a cultural program to raise the standard of living
and to promote Anglo-Hispano good will are common.

Of somewhat more influence during the twenties and
thirties than recently were the Honorary Commissions,
composed of the most respected members of the Mexican
community in a large town. The object is mutual aid and
protection. Since the members are commonly still Mexican citizens, the Commissions stress *Mexicanismo* and work
closely with the consuls on behalf of the immigrant Mexicans.[2] The Commissions commonly are in charge of the
Sixteenth of September (Mexican Independence Day)
celebrations invariably held in Mexican communities.

Typical of an entirely different sort of organization is
the Mexican-American Movement. Basically oriented toward native-born Americans of Mexican parentage, it was
organized in Southern California in 1941 as an outgrowth
of a yearly conference sponsored by the Los Angeles
YMCA for Mexican-American young men. Its Advisory
Council is made up of teachers, judges, professors, and
other responsible civic leaders, and its Executive Council
is made up of youth leaders of the southern California area.
Its potential membership is limited by its early Protestant
background.

Probably largest in membership of the secular organizations that have ever existed for Mexican Americans was

[2] Manuel Gamio, *Mexican Immigration to the United States* (Chicago:
University of Chicago Press, 1930), p. 132.

the Mexican Congress, which was organized in 1938 and disbanded with the war. It was a Southwestern federation of organizations with a total membership estimated as high as 6,000. Its purpose was to work for "the economic and social and cultural betterment of the Mexican people, to have an understanding between the Anglo-Americans and Mexicans, to promote organizations of working people by aiding trade unions, and to fight discrimination actively."[3] It did not receive full support because some of the older people deemed it radical, but it did have some influence in lessening discrimination in certain areas of southern California.

Recently various Latin-American service clubs in the Rocky Mountain region, made up of Mexicans, Mexican Americans, and Spanish Americans, have organized into Community Service Clubs, Inc. This group originated the idea that some of the common purposes of the local clubs—promoting health, welfare, and education, furnishing student aid, and planning, organizing, and rendering social services—might be accomplished more efficiently by co-ordinated groups. It publishes the *Pan-American News*, in English, in Denver. Much like Community Service Clubs, Inc., are the Unity Leagues in southern California, led by Ignacio Lopez. With Mexican-American war veterans playing a leading role, the Unity Leagues have been consistently and successfully concerned with the most obvious needs of the Mexican communities. The Mexican Civic Committee, organized in Chicago by Frank M. Paz, functions in much the same way. Each of these is particularly important, for each is a real grass-roots, local type of organization. If there is ever to be a national organization comparable to the Japanese-American Citizen's League or the National Association for the Advance-

[3] Beatrice W. Griffith, *American Me* (Boston: Houghton-Mifflin, 1948), p. 241.

ment of Colored People, it probably will come as a result of the unification of many of these local and regional organizations.

There are other organizations of somewhat less wide appeal which augment the possibilities of organized social relationships: local units of the Woodmen of the World, American Legion Posts, and numerous religiously oriented organizations such as the Catholic Youth Organization, the YMCA, and various adult organizations for both Catholics and Protestants. All in all, there are proportionally more organizations among Mexicans and Mexican Americans in the United States than in Mexico, and this organized group life tends to stimulate useful activities, to awaken the desire for co-operation, and to help break down the isolation of the immigrant and thus aid in his Americanization.

Politics. The participation of Mexicans and Mexican Americans in American politics has been quite insignificant in comparison with their numbers, but this is by no means inexplicable. Most Mexican immigrants have expected to return to Mexico, and a sizable proportion have actually done so. Even many of those who have lived in the United States continuously for 20 years have thought of themselves as Mexicans temporarily in the United States. This attitude has made United States citizenship not only unnecessary but not even very desirable. Others, in large numbers, entered this country in a fashion which was wholly or in part illegal and hence are unable to furnish the needed certificate of legal entry, even if they did wish to become citizens. Still others, who are native-born citizens, move about so much that they have difficulty in proving legal local residence or are so basically unattached to the community of which they are a legal part that they have no interest in elections and other community concerns. Often native-born citizens with legal residence have not been interested in politics because they have felt that they could have no influence anyway; as one shopkeeper said, "Politics in this state is just two Anglo parties, neither of which cares anything about us. I'd like to help *la raza*, but you can't do it through politics." Still others are disillusioned about their own would-be political leaders, all too many of whom are what the Mexicans call *coyotes* or *chaqueteros*, feeding on the misery of their people, and playing on either side of the fence as opportunism dictates.[4] On the whole, the Mexicans and Mexican Americans in the United States were of little political significance before 1945, save in a few cities in Texas such as Laredo, Brownsville, and San Antonio. This generalization also excludes the Spanish Americans of New Mexico whose political significance was treated in a previous chapter.

Since the end of the war this political impotence has shown signs of modification. Many thousands of Mexican Americans served in our armed forces during World War II, and they have formed the nucleus of a group interested in bettering their semisegregated communities through political action; because some improvements have been made, they have been encouraged to believe that still better conditions can be achieved. In 1946 a Mexican American was elected to the city council in Chino, California, with some Anglo assistance. In other towns, Unity Leagues emphasizing voter education have been organized successfully and their candidates have been elected. The Industrial Areas Foundation, the organization which began the Back-of-the-Yards Movement in Chicago, has a full-time representative in southern California who works directly with voter-education groups. There are now several Mexican-American city councilmen in Texas and several in California, including a councilman in Los Angeles elected in 1949. This was the first time a Mexican American had

[4] *Ibid.*, pp. 233 ff.

served in such a capacity since 1881, and was the result of much personal work in registering voters and then getting out the vote. Negroes, Japanese, and immigrant groups also supported this Mexican-American candidate. This was also a "people's awakening" in the sense that a very small sum was spent on the campaign, with most of the work being done on a person-to-person basis by volunteer workers.[5]

The average Anglo community will accept the election of one Mexican American to school board or city council, and there are many communities where considerable power is potentially available to Mexican Americans. No clairvoyance is needed to see that when Mexican-American political power comes of age, it will seek allies from those Anglo groups already disposed to co-operate, the liberal and labor groups. Mexicans are still novices in the tactics and strategy of minority-group action and politics, but they are learning.[6]

Discrimination. The prejudice and discrimination which most Mexicans meet in the Southwest and West is of long standing. The earliest impressions of Anglos in contact with Mexicans after the Mexican War annexations were that they were wretchedly poor, idle, and given to drinking, thieving, and gambling. These attitudes formed the first basis for the prejudiced stereotype of the Mexican which often exists today. This stereotype helps account for the fact that Mexicans usually are ranked in the lowest quartile on ethnic-status scales, even by persons who have made little or no observation of them. Although there is considerable class discrimination in Mexico, there is little race discrimination, which makes the race prejudice which the Mexican meets in the United States doubly difficult for him to accept.

[5] Beatrice W. Griffith, "Viva Roybal—Viva America," *Common Ground*, X (Aug., 1949), 61-70.

[6] Carey McWilliams, *North from Mexico* (New York: Lippincott, 1940), p. 221.

In general, both color and acculturation enter into discrimination. If all Mexicans are divided into five classes as to color and five classes as to acculturation, those who are V-5—darkest and least acculturated—are treated but little better than the Negro. Those who are I-1 are accepted almost without discrimination. The large number in the middle classes are subject to some prejudice, varying widely with the personalities of the interacting individuals.

Discrimination against Mexicans and Mexican Americans in the Southwest follows the usual American pattern:[7] lack of job opportunity, lack of educational opportunity, segregation in housing, lack of equality before the law, and various kinds of social discrimination. Segregation in education has already been discussed, as has economic discrimination, although concerning the latter it might be added that during the wartime FEPC, in Region X (New Mexico, Texas, Louisiana) 37 per cent of the complaints involved discrimination against Mexicans, and in Region XII (California, Nevada, Arizona) 22.6 per cent of the cases involved Mexicans.[8] Social discrimination manifests itself in a variety of ways: refusing service in barbershops, soda fountains, cafés, drive-ins, beauty parlors, hotels, bars, and recreation centers; segregation in housing, movies, schools, churches, and cemeteries, as well as in public buildings and public toilets; reluctant service in hospitals, colleges, social welfare offices, and courts; and even refusing to permit Mexican-American hostesses in USO's. Sometimes there will be signs "No Mexicans Allowed,"

[7] In exception are the three border towns of Laredo, Rio Grande City, and Brownsville. Here there is considerable prejudice but little overt discrimination. The city commissioners and law officers are as likely to be Mexican as not. Mexicans live anywhere in the city, have no separate schools, and have their businesses on the main streets. It is true that these towns have a much higher percentage of Mexicans in general and upper- and middle-class Mexicans in particular than do most Texas towns.

[8] McWilliams, *North from Mexico*, p. 198.

"Mexicans Will Be Served in Kitchen Only," or "We Do
Not Solicit Mexican or Negro Trade"; more often it is the
less obtrusive but equally well understood "We Retain the
Right to Refuse Service to Any Customer."

In H——, a South Texas town, in 1943 a teacher from
a near-by town gavé a swimming party for her class at the
American Legion pool. The Legion officials refused to let
the Mexican pupils go in the pool; since most of the pupils
objected to leaving some of the class outside, the party
broke up and the majority went home. In another South
Texas town a Scoutmaster and a group of uniformed Boy
Scouts on a hike stopped in a public park to rest, and were
ordered out because they were Mexican Americans. This
is the area where many cemeteries will not accept Mexicans for burial. Staff Sergeant Marcario Garcia, Texas-
Mexican holder of the Congressional Medal of Honor,
was·refused a cup of coffee in a South Texas cafe; as one
might expect, a fight ensued; after which, again as one
might expect, no one was incarcerated except the sergeant.
Not that South·Texas has a monopoly on such discrimination; when a night club near La Junta, Colorado, refused
service to a Spanish-speaking soldier who held the Silver
Star, Purple Heart, and Presidential Citation, another
fight ensued, and this time the soldier was killed. Although some 2,000 persons signed a petition demanding
an indictment of the proprietor, he did not so much as lose
his liquor license. The reporting of such incidents in both
the Mexican and Anglo press stirred great bitterness, particularly among younger Mexican Americans.[9]

During a 1943 visitation of Mexican dignitaries to
Mexico City, a member of the Mexican Chamber of Depu-
ties made a speech denouncing mistreatment of Mexicans
in the borderlands. He gave one case in which an Anglo
killed a Mexican and yet was released on $25.00 bail, and

[9] Daniel L. Schorr, " 'Re-Converting' Mexican-Americans," *New Republic*, CXV (Sept. 30, 1936), 412-13.

another in which a Mexican was assaulted and seriously injured and yet the aggressor paid only a $50.00 fine. After a long recital of such acts he called for a commission to meet with Governor Stevenson to investigate conditions in Texas. A resolution to this effect was unanimously passed by the Chamber of Deputies of Mexico. Governor Stevenson did appoint a Good Neighbor Commission which, while not effective, was a significant gesture, as was the bill to outlaw discrimination against Mexicans which was introduced in the 1945 session of the Texas legislature.[10]

Hart Stillwell says:[11]

I have been a newspaper man in Texas for twenty-five years and I have carefully watched criminal cases in which members of the two races were involved. And if an Anglo-American has served one day in the penitentiary for the killing of a Latin-American during that period of time, I have not heard of it. . . . We can bring ten thousand Tipica Orchestras to Texas and send five thousand . . . good will delegations to Mexico, yet so long as the Mexican knows he can be killed with impunity . . . then all our talk about being good neighbors is merely paying lip service to . . . a joke.

One factor which has frequently spotlighted this discrimination is its application to officials of the Mexican government, particularly consuls and members of their staff, who are often willing to make an issue of the matter. Consul Luis L. Duplan[12] reports members of the consular staff have been refused service by restaurants, thermal baths, and swimming pools, have been prevented from renting property, have been discriminatorily treated by law officers, have been charged double for a Coca-Cola,

[10] McWilliams, *North from Mexico*, pp. 270-71.

[11] Quoted by McWilliams, *North from Mexico*, p. 273. A long list of examples of the differential legal status of Anglos and Mexicans is cited by Paul S. Taylor, *Mexican Labor in the United States* (Berkeley, California: University of California Press, 1932), pp. 167-74.

[12] From a letter dated April 23, 1943 at Austin, Texas.

and have not been able to have a baby baptized in the Anglo's uptown Catholic church. Discrimination against such officials is significant in view of the claim that "only lower-class Mexicans are ever discriminated against." Probably this was also the chief reason the Texas legislature passed a law forbidding discrimination against Caucasians (but failed to pass the law providing punishment for breaking the law).

Despite the very considerable day-to-day discrimination in Texas, it was southern California which produced the largest-scale violence against Mexican Americans in modern times—the Zoot-Suit Riots. According to Carey McWilliams, who was then a state official,

In Los Angeles . . . it was a foregone conclusion that Mexicans would be substituted as the major scapegoat group once the Japanese were removed. Thus within a few days after the last Japanese had left, the Los Angeles newspapers, led by the Hearst press, began to play up "Mexican" crime and "Mexican" delinquency . . . . A number of minor incidents in the spring of 1942 enabled the newspapers and the police to build up, within the short period of six months, sufficient anti-Mexican sentiment to prepare the community for a full-scale offensive against the Mexican minority.[13]

Then came the Sleepy Lagoon murder trial, in which, amid great melodrama and sordid mystery, seventeen young Mexican Americans were convicted in what was the largest trial for murder ever held in the county. Such a trial made a Roman holiday for the press, and it was difficult to read their lurid stories without being convinced that most if not all Mexican-American youths were delinquents or worse. The eventual announcement that the District Court of Appeals unanimously reversed the lower court's decision and freed the defendants came too late as far as the community was concerned. Attitudes, prejudices, and

[13] McWilliams, *North from Mexico*, p. 227.

fears had been built up, and were waiting for release. A special committee of the Grand Jury was appointed to study the problem of Mexican crime and delinquency. This resulted in a police "crime prevention" program involving the bringing in of some 600 persons in two nights. At this time the terms "zoot suit" and "pachuco" became common in Anglo speech as the result of continued publicity about gangs of Mexican delinquents. Thus there were in Los Angeles, on the eve of the Zoot-Suit Riots, a number of coexisting elements: much-publicized gangs of Mexican-American teenagers, a "get tough" police policy, newspapers seeking a scapegoat upon which the frustrations of wartime could be vented, a large number of persons who by their credulity or indifference were adding fuel, and a large number of men in the armed forces who were at the same time bored and excited and who got their attitudes on this local matter from the local press.[14]

On June 3, 1943, a group of 11 sailors on leave reported that while walking through a slum area largely populated by Mexicans they had been set upon by a large number of Mexican boys. On the following night about 200 sailors cruised in taxis through the Mexican section and badly beat 4 Mexican-American youths. The newspapers used this activity for front-page stories. The next night the sailors were joined by scores of soldiers and marines and went throughout the downtown area warning all zoot-suiters to put away their clothes by the next night or suffer the consequences. There was little violence, and the servicemen were not molested by police, Shore Patrol, or Military Police. The next night they set out to make good their threat, beating up all zoot-suiters they found. The police followed behind them, arresting some 44 severely beaten Mexican Americans. The newspapers headlined the the action as being sure to continue, which it did.

[14] *Ibid.*, pp. 235-38.

The next night a mob of several thousand sailors, soldiers, and civilians proceeded to beat up every zoot-suiter they could find, although the group beaten did not contain over 50 per cent who were wearing such clothes. Those so dressed were stripped as well as beaten. The police, despite calling out about 1,000 reserves, accomplished virtually nothing, and only when the Shore Patrol and Military Police were called out at midnight was the rioting appreciably slowed. The Shore Patrol and Military Police prohibited further rioting in downtown Los Angeles, but it continued sporadically for two more nights in the suburbs. In general the press hailed the riots as a salutory thing because of what it called their "cleansing effect," and the Los Angeles City Council made the wearing of zoot suits a misdemeanor! Within a week, Los Angeles had quieted down, now quite shamefaced, to its normal, particular discriminations, leaving the record of the riots for sociologists to dissect.[15]

Apart from infrequent riots, why is it that discrimination—usually completely nonviolent—is leveled at Mexicans and Mexican Americans? Fundamentally, of course, it is injudicious of Mexicans to be a minority, but there are certain specific facts or charges which seem to be contributing factors. For one thing, Mexicans are often dark, and darkness of skin was already a badge of alleged inferiority before most Mexicans came upon the scene. Second, they are predominantly poor, and so suffer from class discrimination. Third, their culture is different, and hence is looked upon as inferior. Fourth, they are Catholic in a predominantly Protestant country. Fifth, theirs is a different language, and when used in public it accentuates

[15] The above account is largely, but not wholly, based on the much longer description found in McWilliams, *North from Mexico*, pp. 227-58. See also R. D. Tuck, "Behind the Zoot Suit Riots," *Survey Graphic*, XXXII (Aug., 1943), 313-16; "Zoot Suit Riots," *Life*, XIV (June 21,1943), 30-31; "Zoot Suit War," *Time*, XLI (June 21, 1943), 18.

differences and may make Anglos feel excluded, fear insult, and so forth. In addition to these facts there are a number of fairly common charges, no one of which is correct and all of which are somewhat commonly accepted. For example: "Mexicans are clannish." "Family life and morals among Mexicans are both different and lower." "Mexicans live only for the day, lack drive, energy and foresight." "Mexicans are childish, improvident, given to producing too many children and getting drunk too often." Actually, few Anglos know anything of what goes on in the *barrio,* and this ignorance makes possible the belief of inaccuracies, misinformation, and contradiction.[16]

A few Mexicans never encounter the cruder forms of discrimination; others like them in color, education, and morals meet with them almost constantly. But touched or untouched, all are aware of the barriers against them. Many of those not actively subject to discrimination are none the less passively so, for sensitive pride frequently will not let them push in where they think they are not wanted. There are few real legal bars against them. They may vote; there are no effective segregation statutes, for the previously legal housing and educational segregation has been declared illegal by the courts. This lack of legal discrimination is a considerable asset, but it may make fighting extralegal discrimination more difficult. "Rather than having the job of battering down a wall, the Mexican American finds himself entangled in a spider web, whose outlines are difficult to see but whose clinging, silken strands hold tight."[17]

Crime and Delinquency. Wherever there are any large numbers of Mexicans and Mexican Americans the local stereotype is almost sure to include proneness to petty theft, drunkenness, and personal violence. Like any other

---

[16] Cf. Tuck, *Not with the Fist,* pp. 94-100.
[17] *Ibid.,* p. 198. It is this special type of discrimination which led Ruth D. Tuck to call her book *Not with the Fist.*

stereotyped characteristics, these may or may not rest on some foundation of truth, and it is the object of this section to present the facts in the case, some description of the actual situation, and the causal factors involved.

Precise figures on Mexican crime rates are difficult to secure. Since the Mexicans are legally white, many records do not distinguish between Americans of Mexican descent and those of European descent. The FBI's Uniform Crime Reports, the most reliable guide to figures on crime, no longer classifies crimes by Mexicans separately. For 1939, 1940, and 1941, the last years it did so, Mexicans were listed as contributing about 2.5 per cent of the total arrests, and they made up no more than 2.5 per cent of the total population. For these three years arrests for drunkenness ranked first, making up a total of 31 per cent of all Mexican arrests; among white arrests drunkenness also ranked first but in a percentage of only 21.5 per cent. For whites, suspicion ranked second and larceny third. For Mexicans vagrancy ranked second (12 per cent) and larceny third (7.5 per cent). Relatively high proportions of Mexicans were also arrested for assault—5.5 per cent as compared to almost 3 per cent for whites; driving while intoxicated, disorderly conduct, suspicion, and burglary were crimes for which considerable numbers of Mexicans were arrested, but very few were arrested for receiving stolen property, arson, forgery, and gambling; 12.5 per cent of the Mexican women arrested were charged with prostitution as compared to 14.5 per cent of the white women.[18] The number of Mexicans arrested for narcotics violations is not large, but is somewhat disproportionally great. A very disproportional number of those arrested for the use of marihuana in the past have been Mexicans; recently the use of marihuana by Negroes has caused some change in the proportions.

[18] *Uniform Crime Reports* (Washington: Department of Justice), Vol. X, No. 4; Vol. XI, No. 4; Vol. XII, No. 4.

In an earlier study, Paul S. Taylor found that Mexicans were somewhat overrepresented both in arrests and in the prison population, with rather wide variations from locality to locality in both. It is his conclusion that this statistical difference is not particularly significant as regards actual criminality because "racial antipathies and political and economic helplessness of Mexicans swell the figures . . . ," and "Mexicans . . . are frequently subjected to severe and unequal treatment by those who administer the laws."[19] In the same report, Max Handman concluded that statistically the crime rates for Mexicans were somewhat high, but that this was deceptive, for the two groups being measured were not matched in socioeconomic status, and the nomadic life of the agricultural laborer, plus the normal culture conflict of a recent immigrant, was enough to explain the discrepancy if not actually to swing the statistics in favor of the Mexican.[20]

It has been a common allegation of Mexicans and those who study their problems that discrimination in both arrest and conviction exist to a serious degree.[21] An experimental verification is given by E. M. Lemert and Judy Rosberg, who studied the arrest-felony conviction ratios (number of arrests on felony charges divided by number of felony convictions) in Los Angeles County.[22] They found the ratios to be: Negroes 7.7:1, Filipinos 5.7:1, Mexicans 5.3:1, Chinese and Japanese 3.7:1, whites 2.7:1. These ratios indicate ease of arrest; that is, Mexicans were arrested about twice as frequently as Anglos on felony charges too flimsy to warrant a conviction. Even these

[19] In *Report on Crime and the Foreign Born* (Washington: Government Printing Office, 1931), pp. 242-43.

[20] *Ibid.*, pp. 244-64.

[21] See Hart Stillwell, *Border City* (Garden City, N. Y.: Doubleday, 1945), for illustrations.

[22] E. M. Lemert and Judy Rosberg, "Crime and Punishment among Minority Groups in Los Angeles County," *Proceedings of the Pacific Coast Sociological Society* (June, 1946), p. 133.

figures do not tell the whole story, for Mexicans are more likely than whites to plead guilty and to receive poor counsel when they plead innocent; moreover, it is whites, not Mexicans, who "know the ropes" and can "fix" a case so that they may plead guilty to a misdemeanor rather than be tried on a felony charge.

Though it is well known that police personnel are rarely drawn from the educational upper strata of society, it is somewhat surprising to learn of an officially published report on Mexican delinquency by a bureau chief of the Los Angeles County Sheriff's Office in which he says:

> . . . the Anglo-Saxon, when engaged in fighting . . . resorts to fisticuffs . . . but this Mexican element considers all that to be a sign of weakness, and all he knows and feels is a desire to use a knife . . . to kill, or at least let blood. . . . When there is added to this inborn characteristic that has come down through the ages, the use of liquor, then we certainly have crimes of violence.[13]

In a newspaper interview this same official told reporters that he thought this inborn trait of bloodletting probably came from or was related to the blood sacrifices of the ancient Mayas and Aztecs. In regard to one portion of the above quotation it can be stated categorically that young Mexican Americans like boxing very much. Not only is it a major sport for Mexicans in CYO's and YMCA's but there are some 2,500 to 3,000 Mexican professional boxers, mostly flyweights, welterweights, and lightweights—some of them champions. The motivation involved is not, however, an inborn trait, but the fact that this field offers a chance to make money quickly, to be noticed, and to "be somebody."

For all immigrants, culture conflict or culture differences are potential sources of disorganization. In Mexico, it is perfectly normal for men to idle on the street corner; they actually are getting the day's news, for the street

[23] Quoted in McWilliams, *North from Mexico*, p. 234.

corner is the illiterate's newspaper. In this country that pattern may continue, and the boys may follow their fathers' pattern of loafing and conversing on the streets; they, however, are likely to get into trouble, which did not happen to their fathers. Moreover, in Mexico, the pattern is to release the boy from controls when he is sixteen, so that he may become a man; this means sex, alcohol, and possibly some violence. In the old country it was assumed the boy would have his fling, get it out of his system, and settle down. Here he is considered a delinquent and sent to a training school, despite his parents' protests that he is not a bad boy.

In Mexico girls are strictly supervised, and some of this pattern is carried over to the new country. Even so they have what seems to their parents to be tremendous freedom, though often it is not—there is considerable evidence that, class for class, Mexican girls are less likely to be sexually delinquent than white or Negro girls.

The delinquency rates of Mexican and Mexican-American boys are usually higher than those of Anglos; whether this ratio is true class for class has not been demonstrated, but totals indicate that the percentage of delinquent Mexican Americans may be double or even triple that of Anglos. For the past ten years the spotlight has been on Mexican-American gangs as producers of delinquency.[24] In Los Angeles, San Antonio, and Denver, these youngsters are called "pachucos."[25] Usually they are marginal persons, lost between the old Mexican world which they do not accept and the new American world

[24] Cf. E. S. Bogardus, "Mexican-American Youth and Gangs," *Sociology and Social Research*, XXII (Sept., 1945), 55-66.

[25] The term *pachuco* seems first to have carried no derisive or negative connotations, and to have been used with some pride by those so designated. As the term came into usage by Anglos, however, it became a derogatory appellation, commonly coupled by them with adjectives like *damn, stinking*, etc. Currently the term, now usually shortened to *pachuc* or *chuc*, if applied derisively (particularly by an Anglo) is an inviation to fight, although it is permitted within the group just as is the term *nigger* among Negroes.

which does not accept them. Wallace Stegner[26] aptly explains:

> The *pachuco* world, a kind of sub-culture between the Mexican and American, is half at war with society. Its core is the neighborhood gang, not the family or school. Its center is whatever drug store or poolroom or street corner provides a handy gathering place. . . . They go out of their way to make themselves visible and exaggerate their differences. The Zoot-suits and duck-tail haircuts, chin-whiskers and goggles, the specialized language[27]— part English, part Spanish, part "jive," part *"pachucana"* derived from Mexican underworld lingo—these are all rebellious assertions of their right to be noticed.

As Broom and Shevsky[28] point out,

> In all populations where the immigrant group is predominant among adults, the strata of acculturation are age structured. The cleavage in the case of Mexicans in Southern California has gone so far that the second generation has become isolated from the parental group but has not secured access to the larger society. The formation of gangs of Mexican youth is an obvious manifestation of this condition.

The prevalence of such teen-age gangs is indicative of the feeling of many Mexican-American youths that they want to belong somewhere. They seek to compensate,

[26] Wallace Stegner, *One Nation* (Boston: Houghton- Mifflin Co., 1945), p. 118; also chap. vi.

[27] Griffith, *American Me*, pp. 55-59, has a lengthy discussion of this language, plus a glossary. She says it is a mixture of anglicized Spanish, hispanized English, words of pure invention, and a jargon in some use by urban illiterates and criminals in Mexico. She estimates that in Los Angeles one-third of the Mexican-American youth speak it, one-third understand a good deal of it, and one-third look upon it as vulgar, illiterate speech. It grew up during the 1920's, reached its peak in the late thirties and early forties, and has since shown some decline. Most words are understood in all *barrios*, but a good many are localized in a single neighborhood. For some youngsters this use of pachucana serves as a hindrance in acquiring good Spanish or English and thus is something of a language barrier.

[28] Leonard Broom and Eshref Shevsky, "Mexicans in the United States: A Problem in Social Differentiation," *Sociology and Social Research*, XXXVI (Jan.-Feb., 1952), 150-58.

through gang unity, for the security and stability which otherwise often is lacking in their lives. Probation officers and social workers say pachucos are not antisocial at all, but are almost painfully social.

San Antonio, Texas, has a population of nearly 400,000, almost 40 per cent of whom are Mexican or Mexican American. A recent study of male delinquents there yielded Harold B. Crasilneck the following conclusions:[29] (1) The majority of the delinquents were native-born of foreign-born parents. (2) The average age at first arrest was 12.4 years, the average age at commitment was 14.7. (3) The three most common offenses were theft, burglary, and injury to a person. (4) Most of the offenses occurred at night, in a slum area or in the downtown area. (5) The homes of most of the delinquents were over-crowded houses or tenements in the West Side slum area. (6) Most of the delinquents belonged to one of the four major gangs in San Antonio. Initial acts of delinquency as well as recidivism were often directly connected with gang activity. (7) The majority were not attending school at the time of their last offense. The average delinquent had attained the fourth grade at his first referral and had not quite reached the sixth grade (range: first grade to twelfth grade) at the time of his official hearing. (8) The average educational level of the fathers and mothers was the second grade. The vast bulk of the fathers were unskilled laborers, and two-thirds of the mothers were working. (9) Two-thirds of the homes involved were broken. (10) Eleven per cent of the boys and 11 per cent of the parents regularly attended church; 55 per cent of the boys and 53 per cent of the parents never attended church. On the basis of these facts, Crasilneck concluded that there were about a dozen interrelated fac-

[29] Harold B. Crasilneck, "A Study of One Hundred Male Latin-American Juvenile Delinquents in San Antonio, Texas" (Master's thesis, University of Texas, Austin, Texas, 1948), pp. 89-92.

tors which could be considered causal in this situation. These included: language handicaps, limited educational background, broken homes, employment of both parents away from home, rejection of children by parents, over-crowded households, lack of regulated social life, economic and social segregation, low income conditions, sub-standard physical environment, the power of the gang in controlling the lives of its members, and the complex problems of cultural contact and conflict caused by im-migration.

Louise Harvey's comparative study in 1949 of delin-quent Anglo and Mexican boys yielded the conclusions that the socioeconomic status of the Mexican delinquents was inferior to that of the Anglos, but not inferior to that of typical Mexican families.[30]   On the average Mexican delinquents had lower intelligence ratings, but there were more of the Anglos who were mentally deficient.   Psy-chiatric abnormalities were more frequent among Ameri-cans.   In the psychiatric cases a difference was noted be-tween the two groups: the Mexican boys seemed to be trying aggressively to meet a frustrating condition; the Anglo boys seemed to be retreating from reality.

The general conclusion which seems most logically drawn from the various studies of Spanish-speaking per-sons is that crime and delinquency are real and serious problems within this group.   They are, however, probably no worse for this group than for any other group matched equally for nonnationality factors such as housing, broken homes, inadequate social life, etc.   No other really sig-nificant variations seem to exist, with the possible exception of the strength of the pachuco type of gangs of teenagers whose uniqueness and social cohesion is probably increased by language and cultural factors.

[30] Louise F. Harvey, "The Delinquent Mexican Boy," *Journal of Edu-cational Research*, XLII (April, 1949), 573-85.

World War II. The Mexicans in the United States have only a short history of participation in our wars, chiefly because few Mexicans were within our borders until 1848, when we annexed much of their territory after the Mexican War. During the Civil War, a number of Mexicans joined with Union troops in attacking Laredo, Texas. They were beaten off by another force, also largely Mexican, under the Confederate flag. During World War I there were still only a few Mexicans in the United States. Between World Wars I and II, however, several million Mexicans had come to us, most of them establishing homes and rearing large families. This meant that a high percentage of our Mexican-American population was of draft age, and since many volunteered, few were in draft-deferred positions, and few Mexicans served on draft boards, they were actually overrepresented in fighting units. Between 250,000 and 300,000 Spanish-speaking troops served in the armed forces during World War II.

In the armed forces they showed a marked preference for the more dangerous and exciting branches, particularly the paratroops. They had a bad record for going AWOL temporarily, but were excellent combat troops. Many fought with the Thirty-sixth Division from Texas, which had the third highest casualty rate among all divisions. Aliens were not permitted to choose their service and many were placed with the Eighty-eighth Infantry, the famous "Blue Devils." In all, 11 Spanish-speaking soldiers received the Congressional Medal of Honor, thus forming a significant percentage of the persons ever so honored. In Los Angeles, where Mexican Americans form about 10 per cent of the population, in 10 local casualty lists chosen at random, about 20 per cent of the names were Mexican.[31]

Unlike Negroes, they were not appreciably discriminated against by the Army, and many of them became non-

[31] Griffith, *American Me*, pp. 256-64.

commissioned officers. A relatively small percentage became commissioned officers, largely because of lack of higher education. These young men were usually judged as individuals and many made Anglo friends; this was the first time that some had met either of these attitudes. These veterans now have a great leadership potential for *la raza*, for they know about the outside world, speak adequate English, are self-reliant, and have no respect for *Mexicanismo* or for "accommodating" leadership. They do not willingly submit to the cramped outlook of a *barrio*, or meekly accept the discrimination which has hampered them in the past.[32] Many of these young men have benefited from the G.I. Bill, and many of their relatives made the first decent wages in their lives, often in war industries, during the war period.

Assimilation. The degree to which and the rate at which a minority takes on the material and nonmaterial culture of the majority is an important index of their adjustment. Such a measure is, unfortunately, extremely difficult to use. Since assimilation commonly takes more than one generation, the percentage of foreign-born in a group furnishes a rough index to the extent to which that group might be expected to assimilate.

In 1910 there were enumerated 382,761 persons either born in Mexico or native-born of foreign or mixed parentage; of this number 54 per cent were foreign-born. In 1920 the total had increased to 731,559, of whom 65 per cent were foreign-born. In 1930 the number was 1,222,439, of whom 51 per cent were foreign-born. And in 1940 there were 1,076,653 in this group, of whom 34 per cent were foreign-born. Between 1910 and 1920 the number of foreign-born Mexicans increased over 100 per cent, between 1920 and 1930 it increased about 35 per cent, and

---

[32] Cf. Tuck, *Not with the Fist*, pp. 220-21, and F. J. Brown and J. S. Roucek, *One America* (New York: Prentice-Hall, 1945), p. 352.

between 1930 and 1940 it decreased over 40 per cent.[33]
Foreign-born Mexicans are by no means evenly distributed
as to states, although the decline in numbers was more or
less proportional from state to state.   In 1930 there were
266,046 foreign-born Mexicans in Texas, and in 1940
there were only 159,266; in California the decline was
from 199,165 to 134,312; in Arizona from 48,824 to
24,902; in Illinois from 21,499 to 10,065; in New Mexico
from 16,347 to 8,875; in Colorado from 13,125 to 6,360;
in Kansas from 11,116 to 5,122; in Michigan from 9,778
to 3,694; in Indiana from 7,601 to 2,160; in New York
from 5,065 to 3,567.[34]   Although these figures are relatively high, the number of persons listed as foreign-born
is an imperfect index of assimilation in the case of any
group of high visibility and low economic status, for any
such group retains its minority-group status over several
generations, and the more so in this particular case because
the older culture is often reinforced by recurrent passage
back and forth over the frontier.

The assimilation of the Mexican immigrants has been
further slowed because so many of them are folk people;
that is, they have a common body of tradition which is
passed on from generation to generation, which determines
much of the pattern of their lives, and to which almost
everyone conforms.   This body of tradition is made ex-
plicit in proverbs and admonitions, and in the example
which one generation sets for the next and expects to be
followed.   The child in a folk society receives his education by experience from within the circle of the extended
family.   Although the individual has fewer choices than
in a civilized culture, life has much continuity and social

[33] Derived from Sixteenth Census, Series P-15, No. 1, June 9, 1942,
Population of Spanish Mother Tongue: 1940.
[34] W. Rex Crawford, "The Latin American in Wartime United States,"
Annals of the American Academy of Political and Social Science, CCXXIII
(Sept., 1942), 125.

change is rare and slow. Not all Mexican immigrants are folk people by any means, but many of those who came during the first half of the major migration are people of this type, and their small folk-world was almost shattered by their immigration. They are the ones who need assimilation most but who are most poorly equipped to acquire it.[35] It is these people in particular whose web of culture is broken and who are forced to mend it with whatever materials are at hand.

It has been observed that there actually are three cultures involved in this particular acculturation: the Mexican, the Anglo, and the Mexican-American, which latter is a mixture of the former two and belongs primarily to American-born Mexicans. The Mexican-American culture acts as a bridge: the new immigrant can acquire it more easily than he could acquire the Anglo culture, which, however, a later generation can adjust to. Most Mexican immigrants rather quickly take on the new material culture's most obvious, external aspects, but the nonmaterial culture is acquired more slowly. This acceptance of the material culture is not always obvious to the casual observer, who fails to realize that the reason a poverty-stricken peon does not have indoor plumbing or an electric refrigerator is not that he perfers to do without, but just that he lacks the cash with which to acquire these aspects of our culture. He does cling more strongly to his nonmaterial cultural heritage, however, in that he prefers his old language, food habits, family organization, songs, superstitions, folklore, herbal medicine, religion, fiestas, and traditional given names.

In the long run, the public school is the chief acculturative agency for Mexicans as for other immigrant groups; for the children it is a direct and powerful one. For the adult, the school is indirect and much less signifi-

[35] Tuck, *Not with the Fist*, pp. 76-77.

cant; for him the agencies are primarily economic ones, his job, stores, peddlers, loan companies, employment agencies, and the like. No other institutions, with the rare exception of the church, make any personal contact with the adult. No one comes around to sell him American history, law, government, and education, no one explains American customs, tradition, or etiquette. In a very real sense the adult Mexican immigrant keeps his old ways because he does not know any other. The best proof of this is the rapid assimilation which takes place when he or his children acquire the knowledge, the freedom, and the pecuniary wherewithall to take on Anglo culture.

In the spread of Anglo culture the social scale plays a definite part. Those in the Mexican-American upper class are usually those in whom acculturation has gone the furthest and who are most nearly assimilated. They are much gossiped about, but they are closely watched, and when they try Anglo ways and succeed, then others soon try them, too. "The 'big people' might be thought of as the precocious children of the colony, venturing where their elders cannot."[36] Thus any sizable *colonia* contains persons who are almost completely assimilated into the Anglo culture, persons only beginning to be assimilated into the Mexican-American culture, and persons at every stage between. As in all immigrant groups, assimilation progresses most rapidly for the children exposed to the public school, so that children frequently are their parents' mentors in the Anglo culture and society. Needless to say, the normal conflict of generations in a changing culture is thus heightened, particularly when the older people nostalgically long for the land of their birth which the children have never seen, in which they have no interest, and which they are ready to deride with typical American ethnocentrism.

[36] *Ibid.*, p. 132. See also pp. 101-34.

Not always is the immigrant happy to accept acculturation, not always does he approve of the new culture which
surrounds him and in which his children are learning to
participate. One of the better-known Mexican-American
corridos (ballads), *El Enganchado* ("The Hooked-
One"),[37] tells such a story.

> I came under contract from Morelia
> To earn dollars was my dream,
> I bought shoes and I bought a hat
> And even put on trousers.
>
> For they told me that here the dollars
> Were scattered about in heaps;
> That there were girls and theaters
> And that here everything was good fun.
>
> And now I'm overwhelmed—
> I am a shoemaker by trade
> But here they say I'm a camel
> And good only for pick and shovel.
>
> What good is it to know my trade
> If there are manufacturers by the score,
> And while I make two little shoes
> They turn out more than a million.
>
> Many Mexicans do not care to speak
> The language their mothers taught them
> And go about saying they are Spanish
> And deny their country's flag.
>
> Some are darker than black tar
> But they pretend to be Saxon
> And go about powdered to the back of the neck
> And wear skirts for trousers.
>
> The girls go about almost naked
> And call *la tienda* "estor"
> They go about with dirt streaked legs
> But with those stockings of chiffon.

[37] McWilliams, *North from Mexico*, pp. 226-27.

> Even my old woman has changed on me—
> She wears a bob-tailed dress of silk
> Goes about painted like a *piñata*
> And goes at night to the dancing hall.
>
> My kids speak perfect English
> And have no use for our Spanish
> They call me "fader" and don't work
> And are crazy about the Charleston.
>
> I'm tired of all this nonsense
> I'm going back to Michoacan;
> As a parting memory I leave the old woman
> To see if someone else wants to burden himself.

The above *corrido* might also be used as an example of the previously mentioned *Mexicanismo*, which began as a solace and comfort for a dislocated group, but which all too frequently has become a flight from reality for the Mexican and proof for the Anglo that "once a Mexican, always a Mexican."

The use of a foreign language is one of the better indices of assimilation or lack of it, and it therefore is significant that in 1940 38.6 per cent of the persons who listed their mother tongue as Spanish were native-born of native parents. This was a higher percentage than that for use of a foreign language by any other group, and is only partially explained by the inclusion of Spanish Americans in New Mexico, for only 7 per cent of those who gave their parental origin as Mexico recorded their mother tongue as English. William D. Altus found,[38] in studying non-English-speaking Mexican Americans born in this country (mostly from California and Arizona) who had been placed in a special Army literacy school, that in the case of these young men "the cultural institution of language had weathered its severest test." These men had

[38] William D. Altus, "The American Mexican: The Survival of a Culture," *Journal of Social Psychology*, XXIX (May, 1949), 211-20.

lived all their lives in the United States, they had spent an average of three years in American schools, yet they were all completely illiterate in English, although some of them were fully literate (Army test) and others were partly literate in Spanish, a language they had not studied in school. Among the factors which Altus felt were most significant in these cases of retention of Spanish were: (1) the propinquity of these men's homes to Mexico and the fact that one in five had spent a year or more there; (2) employment at manual labor and almost exclusively with Mexicans; (3) short attendance, if any, at school; (4) Spanish-language movies and other methods of communication; (5) the common presence in the home of non-English-speaking grandparents who helped teach the child Spanish and who always had to be spoken to in Spanish; (6) the segregation of the Mexican community and its people.

With acculturation in language has come a grammatically interesting linguistic hybridization, particularly among second-generation children. This hybrid tongue is characterized by orthographic changes in words, the use of the English *ing* for the Spanish participle, sentences in Spanish with numerous English words interspersed, the use of the Spanish definite article with an English noun, the use of English words with a Spanish pronunciation or a Spanish ending. A full list would include several hundred such words, mostly slang or words descriptive of things and processes for which there is no readily available Spanish equivalent. Such borrowing is more a matter of necessity than of choice. Included among such Hispanized English words are *ponchar* ('puncture'), *ploga* ('plug'), *gas* or *gasolina* ('gasoline'), *lonch* and *loncha* ('lunch'), *choque* ('chalk'), *sut* ('suit'), *futbal* ('football'), *bisquetes* ('biscuits'), *bos* ('boss'), *ais crem* ('ice cream'), *truque* and *truca* ('truck'), *estoque yardas* ('stockyards'), *chante* ('shanty'), and *butleger* ('bootlegger').[39]

Most of these second-generation youngsters have never been taught Spanish and hence read it imperfectly and spell it phonetically and incorrectly. Their grammar and construction are poor, and it is commonplace for Mexican-American children who speak Spanish in the home to take academic Spanish in high school with little success. The older people say "church is the only place you can hear good Spanish any more."

It should be noted that this whole acculturation process, as usual, has been a dual one, particularly in the South-western states where there are many Mexicans. There are many place names—of towns, streams, hotels, cafés, parks—both old and new which are Spanish. Spanish, Mexican, Mexican-American, and Mexican-Indian archi-tecture and interior decoration are common, are considered desirable as well as beautiful, and are used for the most modern houses, offices, and public buildings. Mexican pottery, basketry, silver work, etc. are common and are in good taste throughout the Southwest. Mexican music is known and liked, especially such songs as *La Paloma, La Golendrina, El Rancho Grande, Cielito Lindo, Negra Consentida,* and others. Many Anglos in this area are partially bilingual and Spanish is more commonly taught in high schools than the total of all other foreign lan-guages. A great many Spanish words have crept into the English language as used in this area and are invariably understood by the native. Such anglicized Spanish words include: *siesta, patio, arroyo, corral, coyote, sierra, adios, sombrero, frijoles, rodeo, riata, rancho, chapparal, pinto, adobe, hombre, mesquite, bronco, mesa, bolero, amigo,*

---

[39] Most of the above words are ones the author himself has heard and hence, unfortunately, are his own spelling. McWilliams, *North from Mexico,* pp. 291-92, has a long list of such words drawn from a variety of sources.

bueno, fiesta, plaza, pronto, poncho, and *hondo.* Some words have been more anglicized, like *vamoose, hoosegow, savvy, lariat, stampede, cinch, hackamore,* and *chaps.*

Naturalization is often used as an index of assimilation, so it is significant that relatively few Mexicans become naturalized citizens. Probably the most common reason for not changing allegiance is that Mexico is easily accessible, and the *emigrés* are attached to it and intend some day to return. Others are poor, and the cost and trouble of naturalization more than counterbalance any benefits which might accrue, for Anglos rarely distinguish between aliens and nonaliens. Some even feel that they are safer not to be citizens, for they can appeal for aid to the Mexican consul if they get into difficulty. Still others cannot show proof of legal entry, either because they actually entered illegally, have lost their papers, or came in as little children with their parents. Probably an even greater number fail to become citizens because of the trouble involved. A prospective citizen must file a declaration of intention; after between five and seven years of residence and two years after filing declaration of intention the alien must file a petition for naturalization. This results in a hearing before the Immigration Service which may recommend favorably to a federal district court. After a final hearing in open court a certificate of naturalization may be granted. This whole process is difficult, and doubly so if the alien is a migratory agricultural worker without fixed residence. The net result of all these inhibiting factors is that the Mexican immigrant is unlikely ever to become a citizen.[40]

It is conceivable that Mexicans might become assimilated to one of our subcultures, as some Filipinos have been assimilated into the Puerto Rican group in New York, but such assimilation does not so far seem to have occurred.

[40] Tuck, *Not with the Fist,* pp. 207-10.

Frank X. Paz reports[41] that in Chicago Mexicans and Negroes do not like each other very much, that there are fights between the children, often where they attend the same school. The Mexicans have moved away from the Halstead Street area as Negroes have moved in. The Mexican-Negro antagonism is visible in El Paso, Los Angeles, and San Antonio. In Chicago the Mexicans are treated like a nationality, and get along reasonably well with the Italians and the Poles, although co-operation with the latter is largely a result of the Back-of-the-Yards Neighborhood Council.

Conclusion. The problems facing Mexican Americans in the United States are many and complex, as we have seen, and some of them are problems not directly related to minority-group status. On any socioeconomic scale, Mexicans rank toward the bottom. Bogardus measured "racial" distance in the United States in 1926 and 1946[42] and found that on a list of 34 nationalities and races Mexicans ranked 27 in 1926; in 1946 Mexican Americans ranked 26 and Mexicans 29 in a group of 36 nationalities and races. At both times, then, Mexicans ranked below the various European nationalities, Jews and American Indians, but above Japanese, Koreans, Turks, East Indians, mulattoes, and Negroes. The explanation given by Bogardus is that

many citizens of the United States simply do not know Mexican immigrants. Others in the Middle West and the Southwest know them only as peon laborers on the ranches and on the railroads, or in the cities as manual laborers. Even they do not know higher class Mexicans. Very little has occurred in the last twenty years to bring out in the United States any substantial understanding of Mexican culture.

[41] Frank X. Paz, _Mexican-Americans in Chicago_ (Chicago: Chicago Council of Social Agencies, 1948).

[42] E. S. Bogardus, "Changes in Racial Distance," _International Journal of Opinion and Attitude Research_, I (Dec., 1947), 55-62.

The average Mexican family in the United States is underprivileged economically, but the whole blame can by no means be placed on discrimination. Whatever the causal factors may be, many Mexican immigrants, and even Mexican Americans, are not equipped to hold skilled or white-collar positions and are forced into the lowest paid, least desirable jobs by their own inability to hold any other. A vicious circle of discrimination, lack of education and skill, and lack of opportunity lead, for many Mexicans, to migratory agricultural labor which in turn leads to lack of education and skill, etc. The very considerable status of many Mexicans who have been able to achieve financial success points to the value economic improvement would have for *la raza*.

Solutions such as this are sound, but are somewhat difficult to implement and are long in process. A much quicker solution has been suggested, "Send them back to Mexico." That such a suggestion has been seriously and rather frequently made should not be surprising, for it has been made sporadically concerning the Negro for over 200 years, was advocated for the Irish in the 1850's, for the Chinese in the 1870's, and at other times for the Germans, Italians, Japanese, Filipinos, Puerto Ricans, and Jews. Although this idea does not have great merit and as typically stated is ethically indefensible, it is more feasible here than it would be for any other group because Mexico herself has been somewhat in sympathy with it, as was pointed out in Chapter II. Nevertheless such a solution is hardly worth consideration; our Spanish-speaking population is increasingly a native-born one with little more desire to live in Mexico than have any other Americans. The civil rights aspects alone condemn the plan and the economic repercussions are frightening to contemplate.

None of the foregoing should be construed to mean that nothing can be done; what is evident is that there is no co-ordinated and well-financed program on behalf of the Mexican group like that for the Negroes. Some organizations do exist, as previously mentioned, but none of them encompass the whole group. There is less motivation for an active program because discrimination against Mexican Americans is by no means as great as against some other minorities. An effective organization needs able, consecrated leadership, and much of the potential leadership in the Mexican-American group is lost because able men either "escape" into the Anglo group or ally themselves with it. As the Mexican-American group becomes more familiar with the Negro, the Japanese, and the Jew—all of which have successful experience of fighting for civil rights—it may well be that he, too, will develop the techniques for conflict now used by other minority groups. Certainly the five years of war put the Mexican Americans ten years ahead because of the veterans' experiences, jobs, and citizenship.

When a number of employed, laboring-class Mexicans and Mexican Americans in southern California were asked if they had any suggestions for improving the conditions of Mexicans in the United States, their answers included: "I live all right. I never thought about improvement." "As long as the people want us to live by ourselves they should give us better streets, sidewalks and playgrounds." "I think there should be a prohibition law; then Mexicans wouldn't waste so much money and they could buy better cars, better clothes, and better homes." "I don't know. I think we should get more money." "I think we should have better education facilities, better housing—maybe even a housing project of our own, and better employment service." "I think that Mexicans and whites should live together in the same neighborhoods, and then Mexicans wouldn't keep so much together." "I don't know." "I think that things would be better for all concerned if all

Mexicans weren't judged by one or two unruly ones. We are all different and we shouldn't be put in one big bunch." Although efforts have been scattered and in general have suffered from lack of funds and lack of staff, some concrete steps toward better Anglo-Mexican relations have been taken. Texas, in 1943, set up a state Good Neighbor Commission which, though aimed primarily at Mexico, did much before 1947 to advance the cause of Mexican Americans; then, with a change in governors, it ceased to function effectively. Further, in 1950, Texas set up a Governor's Council for the Study of Human Relations (with advisory powers) for the purpose of reducing discrimination against Mexicans in state employment, in education, and in business establishments.

In New Mexico, since 1941 the state university has sponsored a School of Inter-American Affairs with a wide program of activities including conferences, a college course, exhibits, adult education, and community services. In Albuquerque, the city government and the LULACS co-operated to start Barelos Community Center, owned and managed by Spanish-speaking citizens. Among other aspects of the center is a program to train leaders for work among their own people. In California there is no state-sponsored program, but much is being done in the Los Angeles area.[43] Included are workshops, primarily for teachers, in the education of Spanish-speaking pupils, numerous conferences sponsored by colleges, universities, and boards of education, the appointment of professional specialists in the education of minority groups, and increased teaching of Spanish in the elementary grades. Co-operating agencies other than those mentioned above include such organizations as the YMCA, Boy Scouts, CIO, Chamber

[43] Marie M. Hughes, "Southern California's Educational and Community Projects Related to Latin-Americans," *Conference on the Problems of Education among Spanish-Speaking Populations of Our Southwest* (Santa Fe, New Mexico: August 19-24, 1943).

of Commerce, churches, the Mayor's Committee on Mexican American affairs, the California Youth Authority, the Mexican American Movement, Coordinating Council of Latin-American Youth, Committee on Inter-Racial Unity, and numerous others.

In 1942 the federal government organized the Spanish-Speaking People's Division of the Office of Inter-American Affairs. While a large part of its funds were spent on exhibits, cocktail parties, lectures, and the like, it sponsored a significant number of institutes, workshops, and conferences, and made a start on an educational program of special scholarships for graduate students from the Southwest. The purpose of these grants was to give Spanish-speaking professional workers, who would return to their home communities to render specialized service, an opportunity for additional training. At the end of a year scholarship holders were returned home to apply the knowledge they had acquired to bettering standards of living among Spanish-speaking people and improving relations between that group and other groups in the population. Unfortunately this valuable program lasted only until 1945, at which time the co-ordinator's office was liquidated and the program taken over in part by the Institute of Ethnic Affairs.

There are, of course, a great many things which must occur before the Mexicans and Mexican Americans are no longer a problem group. At least four major areas can be delineated for attack: economic, cultural, political, and social.

On the economic front, the most important one, some program of controlled immigration is necessary. Thousands of wetbacks seriously hamper any attempt of bona fide immigrants to improve themselves, yet many of the wetbacks are themselves desirable immigrants. A law punishing any employer who hires a Mexican without entry papers might be useful. Wages and living conditions among agricultural migratory laborers could be vastly improved, possibly through joint efforts of labor unions and governmental agencies. A wider occupational dispersion could hardly fail to be beneficial. Discrimination in job placement is slowly declining, and FEPC legislation would undoubtedly be a success for this particular group in three-fourths of the area in which they reside. Culturally the major handicaps are lack of knowledge of English and lack of knowledge of Anglo customs, attitudes, and behavior patterns. Each of these handicaps affects any group whose children regularly attend the public schools unless the group is almost completely segregated. In respect to school influences the outlook is optimistic, for more and more Spanish-speaking children are attending public schools longer and more successfully, and housing, educational, and economic segregation is declining. Possibly Claremont, California, has quietly pioneered one of the potentially soundest techniques for Anglo-Mexican accord: a group of interested Anglo citizens have acquired two sections of lots which they are selling cheaply to selected Anglos, Mexicans, and others who will be helped to build homes because they are interested in living in an intercultural and interracial neighborhood.

It seems to the author that another fruitful technique for improving Mexican-American relations is judicious use of the media of mass communication: radio, newspapers, magazines, television. Though it seems unlikely that these media can be manipulated legitimately in such a way as to change any strongly entrenched attitudes, they might well be controlled so that they do not contribute anything to the acquisition of stereotypes, prejudice, or misinformation, and would thereby make a substantial contribution toward preventing the acquisition of hostile attitudes by those who do not already have them. This action obviously would be slow, but it seems to offer considerable hope for the future.

As the percentage of Spanish-speaking people who are native-born citizens goes up, most of the major bars to political effectiveness will decrease and, if the present is any guide, so will political apathy. Too, equality of social opportunity will probably be slowly gained by Mexican Americans. In most areas of the United States there is already a distinction between upper-class and lower-class Mexicans, with a considerable degree of social equality already being vouchsafed the former. As cultural differences disappear and as economic and educational equality appears, it seems likely that, for the lighter skinned Mexicans at least, social equality will eventually become more a matter of personality than of nationality.

V.

FILIPINO AMERICANS

The Filipinos are an Asiatic people who for many years were subjects of the Spanish crown. During this period there was considerable intermarriage, and Spanish was the official language, the language of education, and the nearest thing to a *lingua franca* in the islands. Spanish culture made some fundamental and many superficial impressions on the previous cultures of the islands, and Catholicism was introduced and made considerable progress in some areas. For these reasons the Filipinos are considered for the purposes of this chapter a Spanish-speaking group, despite the fact that a large number of those in this country, on the West Coast at least, speak Tagalog, Visayan, or Ilocano.[1]

Early History, Numbers, and Distribution. The last Asiatic group to migrate in any number to the United States was the Filipino. Prior to 1920 there were not over 5,000 Filipinos in the United States at any one time,

[1] Much of this material is duplicated in John H. Burma, "The Background of the Current Filipino Situation," *Social Forces*, XXX (Oct., 1951), 42-48.

although during the previous decade they had begun to migrate to Hawaii as contract laborers in the sugar and pineapple industries. After 1920 their movement from Hawaii to the mainland increased and was augmented by a stream of direct emigration from the Philippines. During the 1920's well over 50,000 Filipinos came to the mainland from both sources.[2] Possibly one-fourth of this number came via Hawaii. This was a two-way stream, however, the number leaving the United States in any given year being from one-sixth to one-half as great as the number entering. No restrictions were placed on such immigration and emigration as the Filipinos were nationals of the United States (until 1935) and so not subject to any quota restrictions.

The result of this relatively brief migratory movement was that by 1930 there were some 45,200 Filipinos on the mainland of the United States. This immigration was quite effectively cut off by the exigencies of an immigrant's making a living during the depression. Then, when the Philippines were promised their independence in 1935, a formal quota of 50 was set up. This quota was in effect until 1945. At this time the Philippines received their complete independence and were given an immigration quota of 100, commensurate with the number of Filipinos then in the United States. Because of the practical and then official limiting of immigration, the number of Filipinos in this country has slightly decreased, so that it is expected that the 1950 census will report 40,000 or less.

The majority of Filipino Americans are under 55 years of age. Most of them came as young men in their early twenties or late teens, unaccompanied by wives or families.[3]

[2] See Louis Black, *Facts about Filipino Immigration into California* (Berkeley, California: California State Department of Industrial Relations, Special Bulletin No. 3, 1930).

[3] Cf. Grayson Kirk, "Filipinos," *Annals of the American Academy of Political and Social Science*, CCXXIII (Sept., 1942), 45-48.

This meant a very disproportionate sex ratio, which in 1930 was 143 to 1. By 1940, because older men had returned to the islands and younger families were having children, this disproportion was down to about 7 to 1 for the group as a whole. For 19 years of age and over, the sex ratio was approximately 20 to 1.[4] Hence a marriageable Filipina is a rare sight.

Most Filipinos did not intend to stay permanently in the United States; they came in order to secure savings large enough to set themselves up in business at home, to get an American education, or just to find adventure. More often than not their plans to return have never materialized. Many have never accumulated the desired nest egg, others have failed to achieve the education they sought; they are failures in their own eyes, and their pride will not permit them to return home until that failure has become success. Because they have intended to return home, most Filipinos have sought acculturation but not assimilation.

The Filipino-American Community. The Filipino Americans landed on the West Coast, and nearly all of them have remained there. Outside this area, only New York City has any appreciable number of Filipinos; Seattle, Portland, and San Francisco have sizable Filipino-American colonies; Stockton, California, with some 4,000 fairly permanent residents and a floating population of about twice as many more, is considered the center of Filipino-American concentration, its "Little Manila" being probably the most highly developed Filipino ethnic area in America. Vying with it is Los Angeles, with 3,000 to 4,000 permanent residents, and a floating population of about double that number. In Los Angeles prior to the 1930's the Filipinos nearly all lived on the outskirts of

[4] Sixteenth Census of the United States, 1940, *Population: Characteristics of the Non-white Population by Race* (Washington: Government Printing Office), Table 3, p. 7.

"Little Tokyo," but during the depression there began a movement away from the First Street area toward Figueroa and Temple Street. Japanese relocation accelerated this movement, which is now virtually complete.[5]

In the old First Street area there was almost no community life or social solidarity, the nucleating factors being rooming houses, bars, poolrooms, and the like. The better class of married couples move out of such an area, and their community-making power is largely transferred to their new neighborhood. The lack of community organization among Filipinos is a natural outgrowth of the fact that most immigrants had to become domestics, restaurant workers, or field laborers, and none of these jobs gave them much free time or much feeling of responsibility for community solidarity. This situation has improved since the war as the Filipino American has gained in social and economic status. Now the larger Filipino-American communities occasionally act on a community-wide basis, as for Philippine Relief, for festivals, or to sponsor a Filipino community organization. Often the local Filipino Protestant churches take the lead in such community organization.[6]

Economic Aspects. On the West Coast the chief occupational opportunity open to the new Filipino immigrant was some form of agricultural labor, and from the beginning to the present, casual, migratory, agricultural labor has been the occupation at which the largest number of Filipino Americans have been able to find employment. Young, male, and single, they migrate easily, working as a racial group, usually under some variety of the *padrone* system. They are likely to travel in groups of from 5 to 15, in battered cars or trucks, and gather chiefly on the larger ranches. Although Filipinos are widely used in

---

[5] R. T. Feria, "War and the Status of Filipino Immigrants," *Sociology and Social Research*, XXXI (Sept., 1946), 48-53.

[6] *Ibid.*

agricultural labor, no special area or crop is actually dependent on Filipino labor, nor are the *Pinoy* (their name for themselves) dependent on any one crop. Because of their small size, they are best at "stoop" labor—truck harvesting, grape cutting, asparagus cutting, lettuce harvesting, and the like. They also work in the harvest of peaches, apricots, apples, pears, citrus fruit, sugar beets, tomatoes, potatoes, carrots, and other vegetables.[7] Because they are looked upon as outsiders they may not get the better jobs. In the Salinas lettuce harvest, for example, Filipinos have been used traditionally in the fields, with whites working in the packing sheds.

In the normal working arrangement the labor contractor gets the jobs, arranges transportation, supervises the work, keeps time, and sometimes furnishes board and room. He deducts so much per hour or per day from the wages of his boys, depending on the services rendered. Like any other foreign-language immigrants, the *Pinoy* have not infrequently been mulcted by their employers, by unscrupulous employment agencies, or by their own labor contractors, but probably no more than one might cynically expect in such a situation.[8] There has been some tendency for Filipinos to work, more or less unwillingly, for lower wages than whites. Otherwise their employment usually has not displaced workers, as they have frequently been willing to take jobs no one else wanted. Only during the depression was the displacement of whites by Filipinos an obvious problem. Because to the fresh, immigrant *Pinoy* even the lowest wages have looked good, his tendency to undercut in order to get work has been a real problem to other labor. It has been limited, however, because

[7] Cf. Benicio T. Catapusan, "The Filipino Labor Cycles in the United States," *Sociology and Social Research*, XIX (Sept., 1934), 61-63.

[8] Cf. Bruno Lasker, *Filipino Immigration* (Chicago: University of Chicago Press, 1931), pp. 51-80; also E. G. Mears, *Resident Orientals of the American Pacific Coast* (Chicago: University of Chicago Press, 1928), p. 272.

the Filipino is less docile, more likely than the Mexican, Chinese, or Japanese to unionize and speak up for his rights, as well as because few have risen above common labor. While not expensive labor, they have never been cheap labor in the sense that the Chinese coolie once was. During World War II those who remained in agricultural labor were much sought after, earning as high as $25.00 a day.[9] At the beginning of the war, a few bought Japanese farms. Although the California and Washington Alien Land Laws did not affect them, very few Filipinos have been able to buy land.

To find a Filipino American employed in industry has been rare. In Alaska they have worked in rather large numbers in the fish canneries, and occasionally elsewhere in vegetable canning. But they have been employed in the Merchant Marine in considerable numbers, and even before World War II some 4,000 to 5,000 were in the United States Navy, mostly as mess attendants. During the winter months, and sometimes throughout the year, they work in West Coast cities as cooks, dishwashers, bellboys, elevator boys, houseboys, and gardeners. Some are engaged in occupations serving their fellows in barbershops, poolhalls, hotels, cafés, taxi companies, and the like. During the war many secured employment in shipyards, airplane factories, and other war-stimulated industries. A surprising number were hired by movie studios as extras. This employment plus the number in the Army meant that the war period was the best period economically that the Filipinos have experienced since the beginning of their migration to the United States.[10] Unfortunately most so employed were marginal workers, and were among the first to lose their jobs after the stimulation of the war ceased. All those except the disillusioned and disheartened

[9] Cf. Wallace Stegner, *One Nation* (Boston: Houghton-Mifflin, 1945), pp. 19-43.
[10] Feria, "War and the Status of Filipino Immigrants," pp. 50-53.

look forward to moving out of migratory labor, domestic service, and similar work to better jobs, but discriminatory hiring plus their own lack of qualification makes this a rather unlikely step for most of them. In short, the Filipino American has performed, in his own way, a function in the economic life of the Pacific Coast similar to that which different waves of immigration always have performed on the Atlantic Coast.[11]

Despite the discriminations they had suffered, and despite the fact that experienced, willing workers could make high wages working in fruit and vegetables during the wartime demand, about one-third of the Filipinos volunteered or were drafted for service in our armed forces. In general they were sent to the Asiatic theater of war where they acquitted themselves well. They sometimes did not serve in segregated battalions as did the Japanese and Negroes; all who wished were able to become American citizens easily at the end of three months,[12] but most of them still retained the hope of returning eventually to the Philippines. Currently Filipinos are engaged in a somewhat wider variety of employment than before. Some are engaged in service occupations for their own group in Oakland, Los Angeles, or some other city, some are in the vegetable business or work as gardeners, some are in service occupations with hotels or cafés, and some are still employed as agricultural workers.[13]

Living Conditions. The living conditions of most Filipino Americans have been far from satisfactory. They

[11] Lasker, *Filipino Immigration,* p. 65.

[12] M. J. Bauken, "Our Fighting Love for Freedom: 1200 Members of the First Filipino Infantry Take Oath of Allegiance Which Makes Them Citizens," *Asia,* XLIII (June, 1943), 357-59. See also M. J. Bauken, *I Have Lived with the American People* (Caldwell, Idaho: Caxton Printers, 1948).

[13] In one case in the Pomona Valley in California where a group of Filipinos have settled, they have worked out a sort of gentleman's agreement with the local Mexican agricultural workers whereby Filipinos pick only lemons and the Mexicans pick only oranges.

usually do not form permanent ethnic settlements, but live in the cities during the winter and work on farms in the summer. In the city, in order to save money, several will live in one room, usually in an old house which makes no pretext of being anything except a place to sleep. In the rural area they move about week after week, always living in temporary housing—poor houses, made-over barns, barracks or just sheds. Typical furniture is a few cots, a table, and a few chairs. Sanitary facilities may be at an amazing minimum. Hence, winter or summer, urban or rural, the Filipino American is a slum dweller, with all the problems that such residence entails. Despite all such predisposing factors, destitution and real want are rare. Since most Filipinos are relatively young males, sickness is not the problem it is for other minority groups, and although unemployment is common enough, sufficient mutual aid exists that Filipinos, except during the depression, rarely have been seen in welfare offices. During the early days of the depression large numbers of Filipinos were receiving assistance from WPA, FERA, CWA, NYA, etc. Such assistance reached its peak in 1935-36, and then sharply declined because of the ruling that WPA and similar federal programs were available only to citizens and aliens who had filed intention of citizenship. As nationals the Filipinos had previously been eligible, but when the Philippines received their independence, it was ruled that all Filipinos in this country were aliens unless they had applied for citizenship. Most of them had not done this since they had formerly had almost the status of citizens and intended eventually to return to the Philippines. Hence large numbers were stricken from the relief roles in late 1936 and 1937 and considerable hardship resulted.[14]

[14] Benicio T. Catapusan, "Filipino Immigrants and Public Relief in the United States," *Sociology and Social Research*, XXIII (July-Aug., 1939), 546-54. See also Carey McWilliams, "Thirty-six Thousand New Aliens in California," *Pacific Weekly* (Aug. 24, 1936), pp. 119 ff.

Education. Originally many of the Filipinos came here to attend high school or college, although later immigration contained a much smaller number of bona fide students. As a group, the Filipinos have shown a marked desire to educate themselves, but the number of Filipino students has sometimes been exaggerated in the popular mind because most of the very first arrivals were young men working their way through college. The majority have been frustrated in this ambition. They have suffered from discrimination, from inadequate preparation in the Philippines, and particularly from the need to work.[15] According to Bogardus, only 5 per cent have not had to work, and most of the remaining 95 per cent have had to earn their entire living and educational expenses.[16] For many an ambitious young Filipino the difficulties have been insurmountable, and frustrated ambition has brought discouragement and demoralization. Only a minority have ever thought of themselves as students, but of those who still consider themselves as such, probably two-thirds actually have dropped out of school permanently, and a like percentage who want to become students probably never will enroll. It was during the 1920's that Filipino education was at its height, and in 1929-30 there were 896 Filipino college students actually in school, including 30 Filipinas. Then students were attending 124 different colleges throughout the United States. In 49 of these 124 colleges there was only 1 Filipino student, and rarely were there more than 5 or 6.[17]

Some of this dispersion has been due to missionary scholarships, but not all. Although the majority are nominally Catholic, few Filipinos are religiously active; both

[15] Cf. B. T. Catapusan, "Problems of Filipino Students in America," *Sociology and Social Research*, XXVI (Nov., 1941), 146-53.

[16] F. J. Brown and J. S. Roucek, *Our Racial and National Minorities* (New York: Prentice-Hall, 1937), p. 251.

[17] Lasker, *Filipino Immigration*, pp. 369-75.

Catholic and Protestant drift rapidly away from religion. Seemingly only where they have been welcomed to a youth organization, the YMCA for example, have Filipinos retained their religious interest.

During the twenties and early thirties the literacy and mental alertness of the Filipino Americans was proved by the proportionately large number of newspapers and magazines which appeared. Their lack of financial resources also was amply demonstrated by the short life and high death rate of such undertakings. The most popular and successful type of periodical was the combined newspaper-magazine which contained news, advertising, photographs, and a high ratio of editorials, columns, and signed articles. When the depression cut deeply into available resources and the United States' agreement to grant the Philippines independence cut out one of the major items of discussion, the Filipino press as a whole was unable to survive the dual blow, and, except for a few scattered papers, disappeared.[18]

Disorganization. As a group, the Filipinos have been subject to a full quota of social problems. The great preponderance of young males, the absence of older persons, the extensive lack of family life, and the living conditions in labor camps promote not only restlessness and migratoriness but also instability of personality and abnormal social life.

It is not difficult to see how the members of such a group may be drawn into unwholesome associations and into vice. In the absence of a normal family life and without the opportunity for normal sex relations, often crowded together in small houses or apartments that hardly deserve the name of home, or in camps just a little above the level of insanitation at which they would be condemned by the health authorities, often without wholesome means of recreation, engaged for long hours in tedious work to which many of them are not accustomed by their previous mode

[18] Cf. E. S. Bogardus, "The Filipino Press in the United States," *Sociology and Social Research*, XVIII (July-Aug., 1933), 469-79.

of life—such boys and young men all too readily become the easy mark for the providers of commercial vice.[19]

So the Filipino is charged with immorality—not without reason, for all large groups of young men without home restraints show a greater immorality than the average population. Yet, since this is a serious charge, and one commonly made against the Filipino Americans, it is well to remember that almost every minority group has been charged with serious immorality—the Chinese, Mexicans, Jews, Indians, Negroes, Irish, Poles, Germans, Italians, Slavs, and Portuguese. The following statement, made 40 years ago concerning the Greeks in America, is a good example of the present reputation of the Filipino:

> When we turn to sexual immorality, it appears that the effect of American life on the immigrant is injurious, rather than the reverse. This is in part due, no doubt, to the fact that the Greek colonies are largely composed of young men, freed from the restraints of family ties and the surroundings of home, where close watch upon the women prevents active immorality to a large extent. Through a scarcity of women of their own race (*sic!*) these young men in America are prevented from contracting marriages in the normal way. Furthermore, the liberty of American life in regard to the relations of young people is construed by the Greeks as license. . . . Unfortunately the women with whom the average Greek in this country has the opportunity to become familiarly acquainted are not usually such as to raise his standard of morality or his opinion of womankind.[20]

In actuality the trouble concerning Filipinos and white girls is complex. Their attention to any white woman is resented by white men, regardless of the attitude of the girl. Because of this, most white girls will not risk a good reputation by being nice to a Filipino, regardless of how

---

[19] Lasker, *Filipino Immigration*, p. 98.

[20] Henry Pratt Fairchild, *Greek Immigration to the United States* (New Haven, Connecticut: Yale University Press, 1911), p. 206. Quoted in Lasker, *Filipino Immigration*.

well dressed, well groomed, and courteous he may be.[21]
This the Filipino resents bitterly, for he feels himself
every bit as good as any white. He is lonely, he usually
must seek white women or do without, and he may express
his resentment at the taboo by flaunting himself with any
white woman who will go out with him. This, in turn,
provokes a greater response from the white men. The
prostitute often is kind and pleasant to the Filipino boy,
because it is her business to be so. He appreciates such
treatment and is charged with immorality. Actually, the
rate for sex offenses among Filipinos is close to that for
whites when corrected for age and sex, and the white rate
for rape is higher. Filipino men are uniformly considerate
in their treatment of women, even prostitutes, and many
times the action which causes them to be called "fresh"
would be considered mere friendliness if done by a white.
It is not only Filipinos who, after a season of lonely work,
are likely to seek a bit of night life for relaxation. Too,
the *Pinoy* who can "date" a white girl achieves considerable intragroup social success as a result.

Much of this whole problem stems from the lack of
recreation normally available to a Filipino. He may go to
the movies, play pool, do some reading (including comic
magazines), or engage in the questionable recreations of
cockfighting, patronizing taxi-dance halls, or gambling.
The last, in fact, is one of the Filipinos' major recreations,
whether it be in a professional house in town or around a
blanket in a rural bunkhouse. Many Filipinos complain
that they are "working all day for the Chinese," meaning
that they habitually lose their wages in the Chinese-owned
gambling houses in town. Filipinos also like music and
dancing, and enjoy singing and playing the guitar, mando-
lin, or flute. Spectator sports also enjoy popularity when

---

[21] See also E. S. Bogardus, *Anti-Filipino Race Riots* (San Diego, California: Ingram Institute of Social Science, 1930), pp. 30 ff.

available, particularly boxing. A surprising number of fly-weight, featherweight, and bantamweight professional boxers are Filipinos. Some, but grossly inadequate, assist-ance in recreation is given by various American religious groups and by such organizations as the Filipino Federa-tion of America, with headquarters in Los Angeles. Fili-pino leaders are the severest critics of their young country-men's misuse of their leisure time, and efforts are made to keep them away from recreational places of doubtful reputation.

Despite all the predisposing factors of a causal and concomitant nature which abound in the situation of the Filipino in America, crime is not a major problem. The most common offenses are misdemeanors only: gambling, visiting a house of ill-fame, disorderly conduct, and occa-sional petty theft. Major crimes are relatively rare, and usually result from the spilling over of some young man's volatile temperament. Unlike other Asiatics, Filipinos neither use nor deal in narcotics.[22]

Intermarriage. Because of the rarity of Filipinos, mis-cegenation by Filipinos is in itself something of a problem. The 1940 census reported 7,409 married Filipinos, of whom about 1,775 had contracted mixed marriages, a ratio of about 1:4. A recent study[23] made in Los Angeles over a thirty-month period of mixed marriages indicated that of all the groups involved the number of Filipino male-Anglo female marriages was higher than any other, with Filipino male-Mexican female marriages a close second. Together these made up 41 per cent of all Caucasian-non-Caucasian marriages. In both kinds the median age for the males was 40 years, considerably higher than that for any other group. In New York Filipinos have married

[22] Cf. Norman S. Hayner, "Social Factors in Oriental Crime," *American Journal of Sociology*, XLIII (May, 1938), 908-19.

[23] John H. Burma, "Research Note on the Measurement of Interracial Marriage," *American Journal of Sociology*, LVII (May, 1952), 587-89.

outside the Spanish-speaking group to a greater extent. The American girls tend to be either children of immigrants, girls from the Midwest, or girls of dubious reputation, and in general girls with no strong family ties. Many Filipinos appear to be married to taxi-dancers, fellow women employees in hotels, restaurants, hospitals, and private homes, and relatively few are married to better types of American women. Agricultural laborers are found marrying or living with women of various nationalities with whom they have associated in the harvest fields.[24]

Most states where Filipinos live have passed laws prohibiting the marriage of "Caucasians" and "Mongolians"[25] and the court arguments have been over whether the Filipino, who is predominantly Malay, is therefore also a Mongolian. In California, where most Filipinos have lived, such marriage was first considered legal, and then illegal, the county clerk of each county serving as the judge of race,[26] and then in 1948 California repealed all her intermarriage legislation as to race. That no larger number of Filipino intermarriages has occurred is no doubt chiefly due to the desire of most Filipinos to return home and marry Filipinas, plus the fact that discrimination and social distance prevent intimate friendships which might lead to marriage, and often prevent the social acceptance of the husband. Rural intermarriage seems to work somewhat better than urban, probably because there is somewhat less public opposition and discrimination and because the rural environment seems more conducive to stable marriage than the disorganized area of city slums. In either

[24] B. T. Catapusan, "Filipino Intermarriage Problems in the United States," *Sociology and Social Research*, XXII (Jan., 1938), 265-72.

[25] Cf. N. Foster, "The Legal Status of the Filipino Intermarriages in California," *Sociology and Social Research*, XVIII (May-June, 1933), 441-54. See also M. J. Bauken, "You Can't Marry a Filipino," *Commonweal*, XLI (March 16, 1945), 534-37.

[26] Cf. E. S. Bogardus, "What Race Are Filipinos?" *Sociology and Social Research*, XVI (Jan.-Feb., 1932), 274-79.

case discrimination, language handicaps, and wide cultural differences are potentially disorganizing factors.[27]   There is and probably will continue to be considerable intermarriage.   Filipino Americans now in the United States contain a large number who intend to stay here, and they naturally wish to marry.   They are or may become citizens, and the prospect of the immigration of many more Filipinos is dim.   It has been observed that when the Filipino does set up a stable family life, mixed or not, he tends to appreciate it greatly and to be the envy of his unmarried fellows.

Discrimination.   The fact that Filipinos are darkskinned foreigners (plus their living on the West Coast) is sufficient to expose them to discrimination.[28]   Such discrimination has followed the usual pattern of social rejection: attitudes of superiority, difficulty in securing housing, difficulty in securing jobs above the labor category, refusal of service in cafés, segregation in movie balconies, being frozen out of local or campus social activities, and objections to Filipino-white dating.   To these problems are added the individual slights and injustices which unpremeditatedly occur when one group feels itself superior to another.   There are, of course, wide differences in treatment from region to region, from town to town, and from individual to individual.   When the Filipinos are few in number they are usually thought of as Latin Americans because of their color and the fact that numbers of them speak Spanish.   If few in number and inconspicuous they usually suffer no discrimination.   When they arrive suddenly and in large numbers, unfavorable reports are circulated and believed, and discrimination results.[29]

[27] Catapusan, "Filipino Intermarriage Problems in the United States."
[28] Cf. E. S. Bogardus, "American Attitudes toward Filipinos," *Sociology and Social Research*, XV (May-June, 1930), 469-79.
[29] Cf. M. J. Bauken, "Where Is the Heart of America?" *New Republic.* CIII (Sept. 23, 1940), 410.

The crux of the most active and bitter discrimination and dislike seems to be the Filipino's refusal to accept his assigned place as an inferior. He typically considers himself white, with all the perquisites thereto appertaining in American culture. He has been taught in the islands that all men are created equal, and his pride and sensitivity will not permit him to assume passively the role of an inferior as did the Chinese coolie a generation or two before him. Most incidents seem to stem from the Filipino's conviction that he is as good as anyone else and his consequent behavior.[30] Between 1928 and 1930 there were about a dozen disturbances of significance in Washington and California. Most of these disturbances occurred in small towns and villages and included beatings, dynamitings, and near-riots. Although the pattern differed slightly from one to another, the underlying causes were either economic or social. Economically, the Filipinos were often opposed by local labor units or unions on the grounds that they lowered wages, and they were occasionally opposed by employers for striking at a critical time in order to get better wages. Socially, the most prominent difficulty was the attention paid by Filipinos to white girls, attention which usually was alarming to the white men rather than the white women. In general the vocal objections raised were the same as those voiced against Orientals: they caused low wages by having a low standard of living, they could not become citizens,[31] they could not be assimilated, and contact with them would endanger our racial purity. It is unfortunate that the Filipinos were and are concentrated in an area especially sensitive to the "Oriental Menace," particularly since this concentration prevents the rest of the nation from knowing the facts in the situation.

[30] Cf. Donald E. Anthony, "Filipino Labor in Central California," *Sociology and Social Research*, XVI (Nov.-Dec., 1931), 156.

[31] This was true at the time, but since 1946 Filipinos can become citizens just as can other immigrants under the Quota Law.

The Future. One result of these conditions and accusations was the early demand for the exclusion and deportation of Filipinos. In 1924 Congress declared that they were not aliens, but being neither Caucasian nor Negro they were ineligible for citizenship. Hence they possessed the hybrid status of nationals or wards. As nationals, however, their forced deportation was likely to be illegal, and their exclusion was also of doubtful legality. Of those who sought Filipino exclusion and deportation, labor unions and California "Native" organizations were the most prominent. Deportation and exclusion were opposed by those employing Filipino laborers and by the Filipinos themselves. A third suggestion, that Filipino immigraton be limited to students and to the better class of Filipinos was supported by intellectual and semi-intellectual groups and hence received less Congressional consideration than either of the other two. The solution came in 1935 with a federal act providing for voluntary repatriation at government expense of any Filipino who would return home.[32] No more than one in forty took advantage of this opportunity, partly because of the injury accepting it would do their pride, and partly because such repatriation prohibited their return to the United States. In the same year the granting of partial independence to the Philippines, with the promise of full independence in 1945, helped quiet Filipino complaints and removed their hybrid political position.[33] The Filipino always doubted whether he would spend the rest of his life in America, yet he did not know when he could return home, for he had to have either money or an education before he could return without disgrace. Then World War II in most instances made him make up his mind to return soon or to stay permanently here; either decision decreased significantly the

[32] Cf. E. S. Bogardus, "Filipino Repatriation," *Sociology and Social Research*, XXXI (Sept.-Oct., 1936), 67-71.
[33] They are now "aliens eligible to citizenship."

instability, indecision, and partial goallessness which had been seriously disorganizing factors.[34]

The future of the Filipino minority in the United States is thus slightly less obscure than that of some other minorities. Their numbers will inevitably decline, due to the low ratio of women of childbearing age. Evidence of the Filipino strain in those of mixed parentage, particularly Mexican-Filipino parentage, will become more and more dilute and eventually may disappear. Most of those Filipinos who will remain in the United States will be those who desire to make this their home and their children's home, and such persons tend to seek and attain acculturation, if not assimilation, with considerable readiness. In short, the prospects are that the Filipino group will become a considerably more stable, a considerably smaller group than heretofore, and a more widely scattered group, with a consequent decline in the Filipino "problem."

[34] Feria, "War and the Status of Filipino Immigrants," p. 52.

VI.

THE PUERTO RICANS IN NEW YORK

When the Spanish settled in Puerto Rico it was a small, fertile, rather sparsely populated island. Under Spanish rule it became a rich agricultural colony, specializing in sugar and rum. Large plantations became the rule, with port cities to serve the export and import business which was essential to the life of the colony; feudal overlordship and mercantilistic exploitation were also the rule. When the United States took over the island in 1898, about 4 out of 5 persons were illiterate and the death rate was about 30 per 1,000; sanitation was virtually unknown. Under the relatively benevolent control of the United States, the birth rate continued to be high, but health and sanitation measures cut the death rate in half, so that the population of the island has doubled in the last 50 years. Today, with over 2,000,000 population, Puerto Rico is the third most densely populated agricultural spot on earth with over 600 persons per square mile.[1] Its natural increase rate has increased from 10.9 per 1,000 in 1900

[1] Helen Wheeler, "The Puerto Rican Population of New York, New York," *Sociology and Social Research*, XXXV (Nov.-Dec., 1950), 123-27.

to 18.9 in 1930 and 31.3 in 1947; these figures can be compared with a 1940 rate in the United States of 7.1.[2]

The people of the island are faced, by North American standards, with a low and constantly decreasing standard of living. Since the economy of the island is largely based on agriculture, and since the land area is strictly limited, there is also a definite limit to the population it can support. In fact, the island has reached and passed the population it can adequately support or employ. This has led to a high rate of chronic unemployment, very low wages, and little chance for advancement. The obvious answer to the problem is the industrialization of the island's economy, but its natural resources do not permit any great degree of industrialization. There remains, until the natural increase rate declines, only one other major possibility for a considerable segment of the island's population—emigration.

Migration and Population. Since Puerto Rico is a part of the United States, the logical goal of such emigration is the mainland. Citizens since 1917, Puerto Ricans not only have no quota but need no visa to enter any part of the United States they wish. The present generation is more truly than any other Puerto Rican-American, by culture, values, and way of life; that large numbers migrate to the United States is normal and logical. Between 1900 and 1910 the net emigration from Puerto Rico was negligible; between 1910 and 1920 it increased to 2,000-3,000 a year; during the prosperous twenties it increased sharply to a 1927 high of about 8,000, but dropped to a net emigration back to Puerto Rico during the early depression years; a small net immigration into the continental United States occurred during the late 1930's, and

[2] C. Wright Mills, Clarence Senior, and Rose Goldsen, *The Puerto Rican Journey* (New York: Harpers, 1950), p. 175. This source of information on Puerto Ricans is the largest, newest, and most accurate work on the subject, and hence is frequently cited in this chapter.

by the early and middle forties such immigration had become an unprecedented wave. In fact, some 170,000 Puerto Ricans have arrived since the end of the war, and the present net rate of immigration into the United States is about 40,000 a year. This is a two-way migration, and significant numbers of the Puerto Rican emigrants do return home—probably 10 per cent to 15 per cent of the total. The vast majority are satisfied to stay here; of those who are dissatisfied, probably half actually return; some of this latter group have failed to find the financial promise they expected, others return for personal or family reasons.[3]

In view of the general economic situation in Puerto Rico, it is not surprising that the majority of male migrants come because of job opportunity. This is also the motive of a majority of women migrants, although many come for family reasons. Friends or relatives who have lived in New York or visited there, or who wrote letters about New York, seem to have had the strongest influence on Puerto Rican migration. Unlike the Mexicans, few Puerto Ricans have come as the result of labor contractors and labor agents. The drawing power of the economic opportunity available in New York has been made concrete and personal through the mediation of family or friends already there. Mills, Senior, and Goldsen give the following thumbnail description:

The typical Puerto Rican migrant . . . is twenty-four years of age, comes from an urban area on the island and had always lived in such an area. The chances are six to four that the migrant is white, seven to three that she is married; we say "she" because it is six to four that the migrant is female. In the wage worker stratum, it is about even odds that the typical migrant worked as a semiskilled laborer in manufacturing or processing industries before making the journey. As a group, the migrants, in certain

[3] *Ibid.*, pp. 44-45, 58-59, 185.

socially acquired characteristics, can be considered better fitted than stationary islanders for struggle on the continent. They are better educated; the women are more likely to be in the labor force. . . . They reflect their predominantly urban . . . background.

In many respects, compared with the islanders the migrants are more privileged than average. Yet . . . many of the migrants are women, in a society where women's economic lot is still often difficult; many are Negroes, in a society in which color counts heavily against them; and most of the migrants . . . are without much skill, in a society where skill is increasingly important to adequate livelihood; and all enter a society where the opportunities for advancement seem increasingly too narrow for the poor, the uneducated, and the "foreign."[4]

As a result of the last ten years of migration, there is a sizable number of Puerto Ricans now residing in the United States. As early as 1947 and 1948 some published estimates ran as high as 500,000 to over 600,000 persons. More conservative and reliable estimates run between 200,000 and 300,000 as of 1947, the 1953 figure being probably over 400,000. This number may be expected to rise rather considerably, both because of large continued migration and because the Puerto Rican population on the mainland is largely of the childbearing age, contains a very high proportion of women, and is not likely immediately to lose the large-family pattern typical of Puerto Rico.

Location. Some 90 per cent of the migrants leaving Puerto Rico come to the United States, and of this number over 95 per cent come to New York City. Small numbers have gone to Florida,[5] Illinois, New Jersey, Ohio, and Pennsylvania, but for all practical purposes the Puerto Ricans in the United States live in New York City. Within

[4] *Ibid.*, pp. 38-39.

[5] In the earlier days, sizable numbers of Puerto Ricans migrated to Florida where they worked at making cigars by hand. The coming of machinery displaced most of these workers and the majority either returned to Puerto Rico or went to New York. Today even Tampa has only a few hundred of these migrants.

New York City, the 375,000 Puerto Ricans are found primarily in three boroughs, Manhattan, Brooklyn, and the Bronx; these are the major pockets of Puerto Rican population, but a number of smaller ones exist. Nearly three-fourths of these migrants live in Manhattan, the majority of them in Spanish Harlem, from 100 to 125 Street between Third and Fifth Avenue. In most of these blocks from 50 per cent to 75 per cent of the residents are Puerto Ricans. In the Morrisania area of the lower east side of the Bronx there is a section of some 80 blocks in which 25 per cent to 50 per cent of the population are Puerto Rican. Until 1949 there was also a core area in Brooklyn, but the dwellings in that area were torn down and the Puerto Ricans spread even more widely throughout the borough than before.[6] There are a number of streets in East Harlem and some in the South Bronx which give the appearance of a Puerto Rican city, so common are the outward characteristics of Puerto Rican population, culture, and life.

There is a whole constellation of factors which act causally in bringing about this concentration in New York City, and the various subconcentrations. There are much better steamship facilities and rates between Puerto Rico and New York than between Puerto Rico and the Gulf ports, despite the longer distance. That is, it is actually cheaper and easier for the bulk of the migrants to go to New York than to any other city in the United States. This difference unquestionably accounted for much of the earlier migration. These earlier migrants, in turn, have acted as magnets for new arrivals because the large-family system in Puerto Rico as elsewhere puts great significance in the mutual relationships and responsibilities to each other even of distant kin. Thus a recent arrival is sure of finding a welcome, assistance, and hospitality if he has

---

[6] Mills, *et al.*, *The Puerto Rican Journey*, pp. 22, 219.

relatives already here. So it is perfectly normal for him to make his way immediately to the place of residence of relatives or friends to secure advice and assistance and often to live with them or near them during the first period of readjustment. This cultural pattern helps to account for the migration to New York itself as well as to the specific core areas of previous Puerto Rican concentration. The third and fourth factors in this constellation of causes are ones common to many migrants to New York. Most migrants are poor, and it is certainly true that most Puerto Ricans are at a serious financial disadvantage. Thus they, in common with many other ethnic groups, must seek out the low-rent areas and live there, at least for a number of years. Too, Puerto Ricans as a rule do not speak English well, and like other foreign-langauge groups they find congeniality and psychic security in a group and area where their language and customs are understood and appreciated. Puerto Ricans further follow the pattern set by previous immigrant groups in this country in that when the individual family becomes somewhat economically secure, speaks English reasonably well, and in other ways has reached a considerable degree of assimilation, it tends to move out of the ethnic area, in this case usually Spanish Harlem or Morrisania, into nonethnic areas where better housing may be secured and where assimilation may continue more or less unhampered. The chief exceptions to this generalization are those Puerto Ricans in Spanish Harlem whose presence there is partially due to an observable intermixture of Negro blood, and whose residential mobility is seriously limited because they are looked upon as Negroes and only secondarily as Puerto Ricans.

Housing. It is extremely unfortunate from a housing viewpoint that New York is the destination of Puerto Rican migrants, for New York is in the midst of a very serious, fairly long-term housing shortage. Because of their uniformly low incomes slum dwelling is mandatory for most Puerto Ricans, and since they are newly arrived members of the community, they must take whatever is available—the leavings. In the areas where most Puerto Ricans must live, buildings are very old and seriously in need of repair. Repairs on old buildings are costly, however, and because of the demand for housing, landlords do not have to make them. If a tenant complaints, he is ignored. If he complains again, he is asked to move. There are housing regulations, but tenants are afraid to report violations, for if they do they may be evicted or, even worse, upon official inspection the whole building may be condemned. It is an open secret that voluntary official inspection has largely ceased, for if a building is condemned the Housing Authority must rehouse the tenants, and under present conditions this is virtually impossible. The result is continuous deterioration of houses and lowering of living conditions. The New York Welfare Council reports a case:

> Mrs. B., her husband, and her two children, Juan, 15, and Maria, 8, live with another family. For their own use they have one tiny room at the rear of a third floor apartment. This room is off the kitchen and provides the cross-ventilation for the apartment. It is so small that a single bed and a folding cot completely fill the room. Mrs. B. and her husband share the single bed and Juan sleeps on the cot, "within breathing distance" of his parents. Maria sleeps with the daughter of the other family. Mr. B. is employed as a laborer and earns $35.00 a week out of which he pays union dues, buys his lunches, pays his landlady $8.00 for the room and supports his family. He contributes to the food bill, as the families eat together.[7]

Few of the Puerto Ricans are satisfied with their present housing; they are perfectly aware of the congestion, lack of sanitation, and general undesirability of their living

[7] Welfare Council of New York City, *Puerto Ricans in New York City* (New York: Welfare Council of New York City, 1948), p. 17.

conditions, but they can not afford to pay higher rents, even if better places were available. There are, it is true, certain slightly extenuating circumstances. Except for Negro Puerto Ricans, the migrants may look forward to better housing when and if their income increases. Typically from 2 to 10 families live in quarters meant for 1 family, and the resultant overcrowding (half the Puerto Rican families do not live alone) is serious. Yet the most common additional members of the household are relatives, and the extended-family system common in Puerto Rico makes such arrangements more nearly normal than they would be in the United States, with probably less strain resulting. Moreover, the psychic tensions of this overcrowding are lessened by the fact that some, if not many, of the migrants were accustomed to identical conditions on the island. In short, the average housing accommodations of the Puerto Rican migrants are overcrowded, often below standard in sanitation, noisy day and night, and generally undesirable, but they are not particularly worse than those from which the migrants come nor than those of non-Puerto Ricans who live adjacent to them.

Economic Aspects. Because the attractive force pulling so many of the migrants to New York is hope of decent jobs, the economic aspects of the migrants' adjustment are particularly significant. Most migrants, men and women, expect to be employed; the majority of those who do not are women coming to be with their husbands. When employment is secured the wages are generally significantly higher than those received in Puerto Rico. A sample of migrant families surveyed by the New York Welfare Council found that 70 per cent of the families were self-supporting, about 15 per cent were partially self-supporting, and only about 14 per cent of the total were wholly dependent on relief. A high percentage of those on relief were Aid to Dependent Children cases. Weekly incomes

ranged from $12.50 to $122.00. About two-thirds of the
families were having trouble making ends meet, and half
of them were experiencing weekly deficits which they were
attempting to cover by cutting out clothing and recreation
and decreasing their food purchases.[8] Despite the problems raised by low income, the average migrant is employed at more than double the rates he was receiving in
Puerto Rico. This is one major explanation for the fact
that skilled laborers may, on arriving in New York, be
glad to take unskilled jobs and hold on to them for some
time before slowly raising their occupational level.[9] It is
this rise in money income and standard of living which
consoles the migrants for having to work at less than their
best skill. Both white and colored, men and women, experience this downward movement. The migrants lack li-
censes, tools, references, and transportation facilities, but
most of all they are handicapped by lack of fluency in English. Those with language facility rise much more rapidly
than those without it.

Despite these handicaps, Puerto Ricans do find their
way into a great variety of jobs. Very few of them come
in as contract laborers and very few of them have any work
promised when they migrate. Once they arrive a few go
to private employment agencies, still more go to the State
Employment Service for assistance, but the majority depend upon friends or relatives for introductions to prospective employers. About 90 per cent of the employed
Puerto Ricans are wage workers. Over 50 per cent of the
workers are in the manufacturing and processing industries, and some 30 per cent in the service trades and domestic service jobs. Few migrants rise above the general level
of their first job here, and for those who do the upward
mobility is largely restricted to the climb from unskilled to

[8] Ibid., p. 20.
[9] Mills, *et al.*, *The Puerto Rican Journey*, pp. 71-376.

semiskilled wage work. In short, the migrants are concentrated in the lower-skilled jobs, and their chances of rising tend to be rather slim, so that the migrants both as to industry and occupation are a rather homogeneous group.[10] Specifically, most of the males find work as assemblers of various products, or in the sugar factories. Others become pressers and floor boys in garment factories, dishwashers, bus boys, pantrymen, laundry workers, porters, or work in the shipbuilding industry. Many of the women secure work as domestics, in hospitals, and in laundries, but many are employed in the garment industries as hand sewers, floor girls, cleaners, or sewing-machine operators; considerable home piecework is also done, such as assembling jewelry or toys, making artificial flowers, or sewing. Some 5,000 belong to the Ladies' Garment Workers' Union.

Escape from these lower-level handwork jobs for wages lies, as the Puerto Rican sees it, mainly in the small business. The first thought of many ambitious workers is a small Puerto Rican grocery store, over 200 of which are to be found in the borough of Manhattan alone. Other small businesses established by Puerto Ricans include restaurants, shops for garmentmaking, barbershops, haberdasheries, candy stores, cleaning and pressing establishments, drug stores, bicycle, radio, and electrical repair shops, beauty parlors, music stores, and bars and dance halls. Such attempts to better one's self are most commendable, but it is only too true that the types of business listed above, particularly if not adequately capitalized and efficiently managed, are the types least likely to produce any large income for the proprietors, and most likely to end in bankruptcy. There is little in either his present condition or future prospects of jobs or of businesses which seems likely to change the average Puerto Rican's lower-class situation.

[10] *Ibid.*, pp. 60-76.

Health, Welfare, and Recreation. The Puerto Ricans,
who come from a background of crowding and poverty,
settled in areas of New York which can only be called
slums or slumlike, and hence are subject to all the health
hazards which such conditions foster. In addition to these
they must make a considerable change in climate and culture, and suffer whatever health disadvantages result.
Other than these rather normal health hazards—which are
serious—there is no indication that the health problems of
Puerto Ricans are much different from those of comparable socioeconomic groups throughout New York. It is
to the advantage of the Puerto Ricans' health that most
of them are familiar with the idea of medical care in hospitals and clinics, and that there are a reasonably adequate
number of hospitals, clinics, and health centers available
to them which may be used either on their own initiative
or through the intervention of a welfare agency.

Because they are citizens and because of their precarious
economic position, this group ranks high in the use of social
service agencies in New York which give material relief.
Many have become legal residents of New York, and
those who have not are assisted as nonresident cases by the
city. Because of the extended-family pattern of the Puerto
Ricans, their first thought in time of trouble is the family.
The Puerto Rican does not expect to depend upon second-
ary-group contacts as much as do mainland Americans, for
his sense of family and primary-group solidarity is greater.
There is some change in this attitude pattern as the migrant becomes an older resident, for he becomes more and
more aware of the availability of social service agencies and
their advantageous use by other people, and is more likely
to present himself as a client. One of the commonest
problems hampering the use of agencies and their effective
operation is the handicap of language. Agencies report
that they have difficulty in finding adequately trained

Spanish-speaking personnel, and clients report reluctance to use agencies or their inefficient use because of the lack of Spanish-speaking workers. The Welfare Council reports that a minimum of 38 Puerto Rican agency staff members are employed in the city, but that most large agencies feel they need more such staff members.[11] There is evidence that the two greatest weaknesses in social service facilities available to Puerto Ricans are in handling fairly young children who need adoptive, foster-home, or day-nursery care (particularly to relieve working mothers), and in helping the 16- to 21-year-old age-group, who are in need of a variety of services outstanding among which is recreation.

Recreation for any age-group is limited for financial and language reasons if for no other. The Welfare Council studied 117 Puerto Rican families in one block and found that only 51 of the families attended the movies, 6 used the neighboring settlement houeses, and 1 used the public library. Children in a few of the families went to summer camps, primarily through the efforts of churches and social agencies. At times 5 of the families went to Coney Island or other beaches. Without any question the most common form of entertainment for Puerto Ricans is listening to the radio, and it is a rare apartment that does not boast at least one set in working order. Newspaper reading also serves a recreo-educational function, and most Puerto Ricans customarily read one paper. In the Mills, Senior, Goldsen sample, 16 per cent read no paper, 22 per cent read a Spanish-language paper only, 28 per cent read both a Spanish and an English paper, and 34 per cent read an English-language paper only. About 65 per cent of those reading any newspaper read the tabloid New York *Daily News*, and *La Prensa*, which is not primarily Puerto Rican but does devote space to the island news and news

[11] *Puerto Ricans in New York City*, p. 50.

of Puerto Ricans in New York, far outdrew other Spanish-language newspapers. About 1 in 8 of the readers read a newspaper published in Puerto Rico, and a few read some one of the several small papers published by Puerto Ricans in New York. Over half of this sample did not read any magazines, but over half reported that they went to the movies once a week or more often and only a few over a third reported that they did not go at all. There are movie houses in all of the Puerto Rican core areas which show only Spanish-language films, but both types of movies are well patronized. The conclusion is that the migrants' exposure to these media of mass communication is rather superficial, brief, and casual, and that their motive is to secure news or amusement, not because of any feeling as to the intrinsic worth of the media.[12]

Education. In any country which places much emphasis on education, as does the United States, the educational status of migrants to that country is an important index to the probable adjustment, status, and role of those migrants. In the Mills' sample, 92 per cent of the Puerto Rican migrants were literate, but their median number of years of school attended was only 6.5 years, and whatever education they have is poorer than the equivalent available to white children on the mainland. It was also found that the whites had more years of schooling than the colored, and that the younger persons had more than the older persons.[13]

Nevertheless, Puerto Ricans do desire an education for their children, and there are some 30,000 Puerto Rican children in school in New York, attending over 500 of New York's 666 public schools, as well as many of its parochial schools. As of 1947, in Manhattan, some 12,000 Puerto Rican children were enrolled; there were 24 ele-

[12] Mills, *et al., The Puerto Rican Journey,* pp. 117-21.
[13] *Ibid.,* pp. 11-12, 30-31.

mentary schools and 8 high schools with over 100 such pupils. In the Bronx there were about 7,700 Puerto Rican school children, and there were 18 elementary and 4 high schools with over 100 children enrolled in each. In Brooklyn there were about 4,700 Puerto Rican pupils and 16 elementary schools with over 100 Puerto Rican pupils in each. In the Harlem parochial schools, St. Cecilia's School and Commander Shea School each had some 900 Puerto Rican students.

The children of Puerto Rican migrants are much in need of education if they are to take an adequate place in American life, but this educational process presents serious problems both to the children and to the schools involved; the greatest of these problems is the language barrier. Most of the children who have been to school in Puerto Rico know some English, for in Puerto Rico the teaching of English is compulsory, and in the past English was the medium of instruction after the fourth grade. Yet because specially trained teachers are rare in Puerto Rico, and because the children hear and speak Spanish everywhere else, their learning is slow, fragmentary, bookish, and as a rule quite unequal to enabling the average migrant child to carry on his schooling in New York successfully at the level at which he left the Puerto Rican schools. In addition, in Puerto Rico, there are too few buildings and too few teachers, so that nearly half the children who should be in school at any one time cannot be accommodated. Hence, migrant Puerto Rican children are likely to be deficient both in the English language and in knowledge, and the schools, particularly the high schools, to which the children come have serious difficulty inducting these children into the system. When there are only a few children the solution to their problems is left to the individual teacher and child; when there are large numbers, the ungraded class and the "big brother" system are the two commonest techniques. In the ungraded or vestibule class the pupils are homogeneously grouped and then moved on as fast as their individual progress permits. In some schools Spanish-speaking teachers are used for these classes. In other schools the newcomers are assigned to friendly, often Spanish-speaking, adjusted children who serve as "big brothers" or "big sisters" to guide and advise the newcomers and at the same time aid in their assimilation.[14]

Because their educational background is lower than the average of those with whom they must compete, there is a real need for adult education among the migrants. Many of them need to learn English or to learn to use it more fluently, and many others need to learn a skill, trade, or vocation. Many need to learn the basic facts of child care, nutrition, health, recreation, and the various services offered by the school system; in addition practically all of them could use or badly need help and guidance in adjusting to a new culture, new climate, new city, new set of institutions, new laws and regulations, and a new set of rights, duties, folkways and mores, and new experiences. Some Puerto Ricans learn through the medium of evening adult classes, but only a small percentage of the migrants avail themselves of such opportunities at all, and, with a few exceptions, those who do do so sporadically and with less than average progress.[15]

Family. In Puerto Rico, the family is by all odds the basic institutionalized set of relations of the island. This pattern holds true for Puerto Ricans in America as well. As on the island, the family is what we would call the household, including all immediate, extended, or ritual kin, friends, and those who live in the same abode and share the expenses of living. This pattern is strengthened by the custom that the most economically able person—the

[14] *Puerto Ricans in New York City*, pp. 13-14, 34-38.
[15] *Ibid.*, pp. 39-41.

father or eldest son or daughter—shall come first to the United States. He lives with friends or relatives here, as a part of the family group, and later when able sends for other members of the family, sets up a new household, and in turn later welcomes first migrants while they get adjusted in preparation for sending for their families.

In Puerto Rico the husband is the titular and very real head of the house. He is the cash provider and the maker of decisions, and is not expected to help with household duties. This pattern is much less sharply etched after the migrants have been here a few years. The wife and daughters may work all day away from home, providing among them more cash than the father, who may even be unemployed and living on their income. The economic worth of the wife as well as her working outside the home bring her increased independence. There is also a common belief that on the continent the law protects women more than on the island. This new position modifies the old pattern of husband-wife relations, so that the wife may even share authority with the husband and have her beliefs and opinions respected by her husband. The majority of Puerto Rican men accept this change, but some react against it, feeling that it demoralizes the women, particularly if they are unmarried. That it does is at most only partially true, for among any large number of young persons of either sex living away from home and in a situation in which there is an unbalanced sex ratio, there will be some who will misconstrue freedom for license. This partial freedom which an unmarried woman has may become a matter of regret to many who lose it by marriage, for given a husband who makes enough to support the family, the wife is usually expected to devote herself to her home and children and a small circle of friends, often limited by the neighborhood or apartment building in which she now lives, plus those from the old neighborhood

in Puerto Rico if they are available. Such old friends tend
to continue to see each other rather frequently for the alleviation of homesickness or nostalgia, and for the informal
security each provides the other. Otherwise, relations with
other Puerto Ricans outside the apartment house tend to
be insecure and casual, even though poor housing often
drives social life into the street.

Not only does the position of women change, but as
has happened among so many previous immigrant groups,
the position of the children also changes. Like women,
children are believed to be particularly protected by the
law in some half-understood fashion, hence they are allowed much more freedom than in the old culture, and are
more nearly copartners in family affairs. Children often
know English and know the new culture better than their
parents, a fact which sometimes estranges the children
from the parents more quickly and more deeply than
would otherwise occur. The Puerto Rican family is thus
subjected to all the strains typical of immigrant groups,
yet it remains the center of the Puerto Rican migrants'
social world.[16]

Religion. The Puerto Rican migrants come from an
area where more than 8 in 10 persons are nominally Catholic, and this proportion persists in New York, although
there is some evidence that Protestant churches are win-
ning more converts in New York than on the island. In
any event, in the Mills sample, about half the respondents
said they rarely if ever attended church any more. Ap-
parently there is a tendency at least among some of the
migrants, to allow their old religion to fall into disuse at
the same time as they allow other aspects of their earlier
culture to become inactive. This does not mean that many
do not continue to cling to the earlier faith, a few even
more tightly than before. In the Bronx, St. Anselm's

[16] Mills, *et al.*, *The Puerto Rican Journey*, pp. 97-100.

Catholic Church, besides its religious services, operates Casa Besaina Settlement House and has special clubs and facilities for Puerto Rican youth. The Spanish Evangelical and Spanish Lutheran churches also have Spanish services and organizations for young people. In Brooklyn, St. Peter's Catholic Church offers Spanish-language services and a number of activities for Puerto Ricans. In Brooklyn exist 17 rather small Protestant churches with predominantly Puerto Rican membership, there are 24 in Spanish Harlem, and a number of others are scattered throughout the city where groups of Puerto Ricans live.[17]

Politics and Organizations. Politics does not play a key role in the life of the migrant. The majority of migrants voted in Puerto Rico, but in New York they generally feel little interest either in candidates or issues. As they become legal residents they begin to take more interest, and the majority who are politically active have affiliated with the machine of Vito Marcantonio, which seeks their support and has a number of Spanish-speaking personnel. The 1950 attempt on the life of President Truman by two Puerto Rican migrants was in no sense typical; in general, the migrants are better off on the mainland than they were in Puerto Rico and hence seem even better disposed toward mainland control of the island than do the resident islanders. Other than these somewhat nebulous ties with political organizations, the only other organizational ties maintained by large numbers of the migrants are those with labor unions. Because the jobs open to them are usually in highly organized industries, a majority of employed Puerto Ricans belong to some labor union. Here, too, the interaction is meager and impersonal.

Unlike some other immigrant groups, Puerto Ricans do not have many "nationality" organizations. In Mills'

[17] *Ibid.*, pp. 110-14, 221; and *Puerto Ricans in New York City*, pp. 25-26.

sample, only about 6 per cent belong to an exclusively
Puerto Rican organization, and less than 10 per cent belonged to general organizations. The Catholic Youth
Organization, several branches of the YMCA, and half a
dozen settlement houses are the major institutions which
reach the young people. The Spanish-American Community Council in the Bronx, the Union Settlement Organization, and the new Council of Spanish-American Organizations have been the outstanding community self-help
organizations with 'predominantly Puerto Rican constituents, and though their activities have been valuable—
particularly the block-organization activities of the Union
Settlement Organization—they have reached only a small
number of the migrants. There seems no particular likelihood that Puerto Rican organizations will increase very
rapidly. The culture of the island does not stress organizational activity, much of that type of need being met by
the extended-family system. Within the migrant group
there are definite class feelings, and, too, the most successful migrants who would be most interested and active tend
to move out of the Puerto Rican areas and to relate themselves to non-Puerto Rican organizations in the new area.[18]

Race and Discrimination. In Puerto Rico there is no
real race prejudice as known in the United States, but
many who are dark are self-conscious about their color and
sometimes feel insecure; those whose skin is light feel
more secure. In general, problems concerning color are
individual problems rather than racial problems, for everyone is first an individual and only second a member of a
particular racial group. Racial discrimination does occur
on the island, but it is almost entirely social in character
and likely to be mixed with class discrimination. Among

[18] Mills, *et al., The Puerto Rican Journey,* pp. 105-10; and *Puerto
Ricans in New York City,* pp. 26-32. This latter reference discusses in some
detail the activities of the Union Settlement Organization, and of various
religiously oriented groups.

Puerto Ricans there are three recognized Negro-white groups: the whites, all of whose characteristics are Caucasoid; the Negroes, who have obvious and outstanding Negroid characteristics (although they are rarely pure Negroid); and the *grifos*, most of whose racial characteristics are Caucasoid, but who do have one or two marks of Negro ancestry. On the island, each group has a different status, the *grifos* being intermediate. Both on the island and among the migrants the number of whites is over one and one-half times larger than that of the other two groups together.

The tripartite grouping used on the island does not fit the bipartite one used on the continent, and this disharmony has serious effects on the *grifo* group and fairly frequent if somewhat less serious effects on the other two groups. The white group is likely, in actuality, to be dark by Anglo-Saxon standards and hence sometimes to experience prejudice and discrimination from white Americans. The descent from a group which discriminates to a group discriminated against is likely to be a disorganizing one, but it is less so because of the possibility of raising one's status or that of one's children by achieving assimilation and financial security. For the Negroid migrant there are difficulties, too. He was recognized on the island as a Negro and is so recognized here, but the disabilities and frustrations of such denomination are far greater here, and many Negroid Puerto Ricans suffer serious shock as the result of the normal treatment they receive at the hands of American whites. More seriously disorganizing than either of the above relations is the new status of the *grifo*. He had, on the island, a position above that of the Negro; on the mainland he not only loses that status and is treated by both Negroes and whites as a Negro, but he suffers from prejudice and discrimination to which he is doubly sensitive and which he feels is doubly unjust, so that his disorganization and frustration are the greater. The white migrants and the lightest *grifos* make every attempt to dissociate themselves from Negroes, to remain different from them; among other ways this takes the form of an exaggerated emphasis on being classed as *Spanish* Americans. In some sections of the city there is overt conflict between American Negroes and Puerto Ricans because neither wishes to be identified with the other; in other sections, however, the two groups get along amicably.

Whatever their color, Puerto Ricans are subjected to prejudice and discrimination and do feel it. In Mills' sample, the majority of migrants felt that they were not liked by Americans and returned that antagonism. Men were less likely to feel subjected to dislike than women, and the *grifo* group expressed the strongest feelings and was the most antagonistic to Americans. In the sample, 34 per cent of the men and 28 per cent of the women felt that "all or many" Americans in New York believed that Puerto Ricans were inferior; 12 per cent of the men and 13 per cent of the women said "none" held this belief. In stating why they thought Americans disliked Puerto Ricans, only 8 per cent of the men and 6 per cent of the women gave a personal experience of discrimination as the answer; a considerable majority of both either referred to experiences reported by others or reiterated opinions such as, "They don't like us," etc. Despite all this, discrimination is sufficiently less against Puerto Ricans than against Negroes that some light Negroes in Harlem cultivate Spanish phrases and a Spanish accent so as to be taken for Spanish Americans.[19]

Disorganization. Whenever any of the important factors in the life-organization and adjustment of an individual are disturbed, a degree of personal disorganization is likely to ensue. If personal disorganization is at all

---

[19] Mills, *et al.*, *The Puerto Rican Journey*, pp. 126-34.

widespread in the group, some degree of social disorganization also results. Disorganization of either sort may
result from a multiplicity of interacting factors, and may
indicate itself in a variety of ways, as in the case of the
Puerto Ricans in New York. Although the Puerto Rican
is a citizen, as far as adjustment is concerned he is a for-
eigner; climate, customs, job, language, living conditions,
social organization, and even his relationship with other
racial groups—all are different from what he has been
accustomed to. His failure to make a satisfactory adjustment in any of these areas encourages both personal and
social disorganization. Various degrees of disorganization
manifest themselves in random, erratic behavior, aimless-
ness and inertia, neuroses and psychoses, delinquency and
crime, excessive use of alcohol and narcotics, and in varying
degrees of restlessness, malaise, conflict, emotional instability, and either amorphous or specific dissatisfactions with
life as the disorganized person sees it. Warren Brown has
indicated that the typical Puerto Rican personality is more
emotional in nature than is average on the mainland; such
emotionality may be considered as a potentially predisposing factor toward disorganization under pressure.[20]

Seriously overcrowded living conditions have been
found to be related to disorganization. As has been said,
the housing of Puerto Rican families ranges from fair to
the poorest in the city, and so is a predisposing factor. The
sudden urbanization of some has often been a further disorganizing factor, even resulting in "slum shock."

The family is normally an important organizing force,
but overcrowding or lack of privacy may cause a breakdown
of this function. Moreover, the Puerto Rican family is
itself seriously subject to disorganization, for the large-
family system and its patriarchal authority both tend to

[20] Warren Brown, "The Communal and Individual Personality Structure
of the Puerto Rican in New York," paper delivered before the 1949 annual
meeting of the American Anthropological Association.

break down after immigration to New York, and the decline of the institution as an agency of security, response, and social control contributes greatly to the disorganization found among Puerto Ricans. Part of this constellation of interacting factors is the care of many children by day nurseries or by neighbor women. The Puerto Rican woman often works outside the home, either because of the husband's low wages, her own ability to find work when he cannot, or because there is no male breadwinner available. Thus a considerable number of young children are left without their mother's care during the day. Such a situation is both an evidence of and a predisposing factor toward family and personal disorganization. One of the outgrowths of disorganization of the family is delinquency, and there is some evidence that Puerto Rican youngsters have a significantly high delinquency rate but that the delinquency is usually of a relatively mild type, and often closely associated with the activity of gangs, the bulk of whose activity is not delinquent.[21] Probably of most importance in Puerto Rican delinquency is the fact that so many live in delinquency areas where there are collected in one spot many of the conditions usually associated with high delinquency: overcrowding, lack of leadership, lack of recreation, lack of child-care facilities, vice, poverty, unemployment, and the presence of disorganized and derelict individuals and of organized criminal gangs. It is an optimistic note that most criminologists agree not only on the significance of delinquency areas in the genesis and etiology of delinquency, but also that when a group occupying such an area moves out of the area into better surroundings the delinquency rate drops to the norm for the new area. In the meantime juvenile authorities, settlement houses, and groups like the YMCA and CYO do what they can to ameliorate the situation.

[21] Erwin Schepses, "Puerto Rican Delinquent Boys in New York City," *Social Service Review*, XXIII (March, 1949), 51-56.

The economic situation of the bulk of Puerto Ricans is another factor which potentially increases disorganization. In a competitive society such as ours, where status comes to a considerable extent from incomes and possessions, the fact that the Puerto Rican migrant is often at the bottom of the economic scale is likely to lower the threshold for disorganization. If he succeeds in getting a job, the Puerto Rican finds his dollar wages much higher than they were before he migrated. This is counterbalanced by the likelihood that he is now doing lower-level work, and that his wants will increase and outstrip his new income. The need for the wife to work—possibly earning more than the husband—adds to the instability of the patriarchal type of family. High rates of relief may indicate freedom from serious material want, but they do not indicate freedom from the mental conflicts, loss of status, and lack of independence which often stem from receiving relief.

Finally, for some Puerto Ricans, the problem of color is a seriously disorganizing factor to which some of them react in an almost pathological manner. Many individuals whose status has changed because of the different classification applied in New York are very bitter, and oftentimes their reactions can adequately be described only in terms of disorganization or neurosis.

Assimilation. One of the more commonly used indices of whether or not an immigrant group is getting along well is its assimilation. For generations a common goal has been the Americanization of immigrants, and since most of the Puerto Ricans seem likely to become permanent residents, their assimilation is some index of their successful adjustment. The historic assimilative pattern on the East Coast has been for the immigrant group to settle in an ethnic area in the low-rent, slum section and there to reproduce, for something like a generation, the culture patterns of the old country. Many of the younger people and later many

of the older people gradually move away to undifferen-
tiated housing areas, leaving most of the outward marks of
the old culture behind, until the area, as an ethnic area, no
longer exists. It seems that the Puerto Ricans are following this traditional pattern. The semighettos of Spanish
Harlem and Morrisania in the Bronx serve as transition
places, being culturally somewhere between Puerto Rico
and the United States, partaking partially of the culture
of each. Here the newly arrived immigrant is cushioned
against the full impact of the new way of life in which he
may gradually come to participate. His social world, at
first bounded by the household, the apartment house, and
the street, slowly expands.

The assimilation of Puerto Ricans is hindered, in New
York at least, by the absence of concrete, homogeneous
norms to which to adjust. There is neither the clear pattern to which to conform nor the social controls conducive
to conformity that might be found in a Midwestern town.
In this connection Mills, Senior, and Goldsen suggest as a
minimum definition for Puerto Rican adaptation "inconspicuous functioning with psychic contentment." "The
adjusted man in a society of homogeneous norms is inconspicuous by virtue of being like all other people and hence
not socially visible among them. In a society with no such
homogeneous norms, but with many different social types,
the individual can be inconspicuous only in terms of formal
common denominators.[22] On this basis the immigrant who
acquires facility in English, whose dress, habits, and customs fall within the rather broad range of normality for
New York City, who stays out of trouble, and who is able
to make this adjustment without serious personal disorganization is well on the way toward adaptation and
assimilation.

It has long been accepted that a basic factor in the

[22] Mills, *et al.*, *The Puerto Rican Journey*, p. 141.

adjustment or assimilation of an immigrant is his language proficiency. On this basis it is significant that some 60 per cent of the Puerto Rican migrants arrive with a totally inadequate comprehension of English. This inadequacy means that they cannot function either inconspicuously or with a high degree of psychic contentment; it means a limited use of educational, health, recreational, economic, religious, and welfare facilities, and a limited ability to understand even the mass media of communication which transmit the mass culture of our society. For these people there is perforce a limited use of newspapers, radio, movies, and magazines, except as these use the Spanish language. Language deficiencies prevent even this external type of participation in America's mass culture. But this condition does improve, for children must learn English at school; they then become the interpreters and even teachers at home. Employment, although there are variations, seems to increase significantly both language facility and motivation for learning the language. Increased income increases the potential for participation in mass culture, and the whole process is rapidly accelerated if the family moves out of the ethnic area. There seems no reason to assume that Puerto Ricans will remain handicapped by language any longer than previous comparable immigrant groups.

One common problem of assimilation—citizenship—is no bar to the Puerto Rican. He is already a United States citizen and he becomes a full citizen of a city and a state in the same way an Iowan moving to Chicago would, i.e., after living there long enough to meet minimum residence requirements. Like other immigrants, however, his opportunity for assimilation is restricted by his foreign culture, language, and his low economic status and lack of occupational diversity. This restriction is particularly true of the women, whose orbit, like that of all

Latin women, is likely to be a much more limited one than that of the men. Even women who work, and who thus have more of a chance than housewives to be exposed to American culture, actually are exposed to a very small sector of it.[23] This is important because there are more women than men in the Puerto Rican migration.

The most serious single difficulty for some Puerto Ricans is the matter of race. About one-third of the migrants are colored by mainland standards; they cannot rise as easily or as far as the noncolored, and their motivation to adjust and assimilate is weakened by the attitude toward their color. Those who in Puerto Rico were *grifos* seem to be the least adapted of all, and their adjustments seem to be more difficult to make than are those of the other two color-groups. The *grifos* do not want to be identified with the Negro group and are unwilling to be considered a part of the Negro community, yet that is the only community willing to accept them. Some *grifos* have found that by stressing their foreignness, by speaking Spanish in public, and by otherwise indicating that they are not American Negroes, they can occasionally achieve objectives which otherwise would be denied them. Whatever the practical value of such a procedure in an opportunistic sense, the net effect is to hamper assimilation seriously as well as to provide no fundamental solution or adjustment to the racial problems besetting such an individual. In some areas of Harlem there is serious and almost continuous friction between Negroes and Puerto Ricans, neither wishing to be identified with the other and each transferring to the other the aggression they feel against the dominant white group.

In all fairness, any discussion of assimilation, particularly if there is implicit in it, as in the above, the idea that assimilation is desirable, should mention the concept of

[23] *Ibid.*, p. 89.

cultural pluralism. This relatively new approach to the problems of divergent cultures postulates that a temporary selective heterogeneity is the best avenue of approach to an ultimately larger homogeneity and that every culture has many valuable aspects which should be retained by the immigrant group or even incorporated into the larger culture—the goal being progressively more tolerant integration of diverse cultural tendencies. Assimilation, in this view, would not be absorption but integration with mutual give and take, each hybridization making the total stronger, the strength coming through co-operative division of labor by unlike units rather than through homogeneity. Though the theory of cultural pluralism is probably at least as socially valid as the older theory of Americanization, the discussion as far as the Puerto Ricans is concerned is largely an academic one, for their adjustment in this and the next generation must be to the currently held concept of Americanization.

Solution or Amelioration of Special Problems. When over 200,000 persons leave a small country in a ten-year period, there must be some significant expulsive forces at work. As we have seen, there are such forces in Puerto Rico, and in a very real sense the best long-run solution for problems concerning the Puerto Ricans is to improve the situation in Puerto Rico itself so that there is no motivation for more Puerto Ricans to leave. This is part of a long-range program already under way, and as this program begins to bear fruit it is logical to expect a decline in Puerto Rican immigration to the mainland. In the meantime, the wave of migration continues, and the city of New York does not have sufficient houses, hospitals, schools, recreation facilities and welfare facilities to provide adequately for this influx of population. Puerto Ricans have, and should continue to have, the right to settle anywhere on the mainland they choose. Before they migrate, however, they should be fully informed as to the housing, jobs, working conditions, and possibility of successful integration in each area. An attempt should be made to direct the migrants to that area currently most suitable for their settlement, and that area should be prepared ahead of time for the arrival of the migrants and whatever repercussions may arise therefrom. In short, within the bounds of individual freedom, whatever can be done to change the present unplanned migration to an organized one, planned to serve the best interests of all concerned, should be done. Such a program would certainly prevent some of the serious human problems now occurring. Some temporary alleviation of the economic stresses of agricultural laborers on the island may occur through the newly inaugurated program of contract farm labor. Under a plan much like that under which Mexican laborers have been used in labor-short areas, Puerto Rican contract workers have begun to come to the mainland for the harvest season. In 1952 some 12,500 such laborers worked in 11 states and with over 15 different kinds of crops. They nearly all fly over, and pay their own transportation ($65 to New York). By contract they may not be subjected to racial or ethnic discrimination, and must be permitted to work in racially mixed units. At the end of their contract they fly back to Puerto Rico. For those who come to the mainland permanently, the migration division of the Puerto Rican Labor Department maintains local offices in New York and Chicago to help locate jobs, to work with employees, and to work with other agencies in smoothing out the fitting-in process for the immigrant.

In the meantime, most of the 300,000 Puerto Ricans on the mainland do have problems and difficulties, many of which are subject to solution or amelioration if properly handled. The deplorable housing of many of the Puerto Ricans is a function of the present overcrowding and un-

derhousing characteristic of New York City as a whole.
Two possibilities for amelioration of this problem are immediately apparent and actually are in operation to some
degree: slum clearance and relocation. As houses in slum
areas are demolished and housing projects of at least equal
size set up in their place, the housing situation improves,
and as the general housing improves, housing for Puerto
Ricans may also be expected to improve. It has been normal for other immigrant groups who have lived in ethnic
slum areas to relocate themselves gradually in better housing in nonethnic areas. This the Puerto Ricans have already begun, and the movement might be augmented if
the proper authorities were to make available special information for Puerto Ricans ready to make such a move.

Many of the problems of Puerto Ricans stem from
poverty, which in turn may stem from lack of employment,
underemployment, or employment at unskilled labor.
Giving full information (in Spanish) on job opportunities
to Puerto Ricans would help; information to the press and
to employers concerning the skills many Puerto Ricans
bring with them and the highly skilled positions some of
them now hold should help counteract the preconception
of some employers that Puerto Ricans are fit only for
unskilled labor. Of the utmost importance is the need for
as rapid as possible an increase in the Puerto Ricans' com-
mand of the English language, for ignorance of it alone is
one of the most significant economic stumbling blocks for
Puerto Rican workers. Acquiring such language facility
means adult education; both the New York school system
and some of the settlement houses are engaged in this
work, but a greater motivation on the part of the Puerto
Ricans seems needed if the problem is to be resolved within
the present mature generation. Special training in occupational skills should offer some level for improving the
economic position of the Puerto Ricans, but no large-scale

retraining program is feasible until we are able to forecast more accurately than now what job demands will be in the next twenty years.

The area in which the greatest opportunity seems to exist is the education of Puerto Rican children. Many of the qualities which are desirable in Puerto Rican adults, but which it is not now possible to teach them, are the normally expected products of a regular high-school education. The language problem, for example, is no handicap to one who has gone through the public school system. The process we call Americanization is both a goal and a by-product of the public schools. Vocational education, frequently not feasible for adults, may come easily during the course of a high-school education. Unfortunately, most of the present group of Puerto Rican children had some portion of their schooling on the island, and the transition to the mainland public school is a difficult one. As has been mentioned, some schools do use vestibule classes, orientation classes, and "big brother" systems to help induct the newcomer. More study is needed in the best methods of helping pupils of this type, as is a greater effort on the part of the various schools to put these methods into practice.

Few child-care agencies serve the Puerto Ricans. More prenatal care, infant and child-health care, and nurseries of various types are needed. Recreation centers are rare, and much could be done by transforming vacant lots used by gangs for lawless or destructive activities into supervised playgrounds. Even the services available are not satisfactorily used; the Puerto Ricans need information on local agencies about their purposes and goals and the methods by which such agencies' services may be utilized. The Welfare Council of New York has recognized the existence of these needs. It recommends the use of Spanish-speaking personnel by all agencies serving Puerto Ricans and the establishment of joint programs of public and privately supported agencies working through a center which would include family case work, recreation, classes in English, discussion groups and forums, with a Spanish-speaking executive director.[24]

Finally, if the Puerto Rican migrants are to achieve a satisfactory adjustment to their new life, not only they but the people of the communities in which or near which they live must bear the burden. A process of education of the native population, with its goal the building of a local understanding of Spanish culture, is most desirable. This would include some knowledge of Spanish language, food, family life, customs, and entertainment. Much of it could be accomplished by intercultural education programs in the schools—the recognition that of the varying ways of doing a thing or of defining a situation, not one but several may be useful, pleasant, and beneficial. The Puerto Ricans are the only immigrants to arrive since the formulation of the sociological knowledge gathered from the study of previous immigrant groups; the prospects for the Puerto Ricans' rapid and successful adjustment therefore should be greater than those for any previous comparable group.

[24] *Puerto Ricans in New York City*, p. 43.

APPENDIX I

LOS HERMANOS PENITENTES: A CASE STUDY OF THE CULTURAL SURVIVAL OF FLAGELLATION

The idea of flagellation as a means of grace is an old one in the history of religion. The ancient Egyptians sometimes flogged themselves in honor of Isis; Spartans were whipped before the altar of Artemis Orthia; Roman women suffered ritual scourging during the Lupercalia; toward the end of the eleventh century Cardinal Damian advocated self-flagellation as a penance and acquired a following. St. Anthony of Padua, in the thirteenth century, founded the first fraternity for regular and public self-whipping as a religious ceremony, and before the end of the thirteenth century it is reported that in Perugia, Italy, rich and poor walked with leather whips through the streets whipping themselves until they drew blood from their tortured bodies, singing at the same time penitential hymns and entreating mercy of God. The movement spread from Italy to Bavaria, Bohemia, Austria, Hungary,

Poland, Germany, and as late as the sixteenth century existed in France and Spain, despite the serious objections of the Church.

About 500 years ago there was founded in Spain the lay order of *Los Hermanos Penitentes* ("The Penitent Brothers"). It was not a flagellant society but a fraternity of men of good morals who met for religious study. This order was brought to Mexico by the Franciscan Friars during the sixteenth century and officially called by them the Lay Third Order of the Franciscans. Within a century it was brought to what is now New Mexico and southern Colorado by them and by some of the followers of the *Conquistadores,* who were previous members. The first recorded public penance in this area was performed by explorer Juan de Oñate and his men in 1594. A manuscript in the cathedral at Santa Fe, dated 1794, states that the order has been in existence "since the beginning of the Re-Conquest of this province."[1]

No bishop visited the area after 1760, and most of the Franciscan Friars were expelled in 1828 by the Mexican Revolutionary Government. Even before the departure of the Franciscans the isolated Spanish-American villages had come to rely upon themselves and their brotherhoods for the performance of many religious rites. Control of the Penitentes quickly and definitely passed from the hands of Church officials to local lodge masters. No real objection was raised locally to any form of worship practiced by the Penitentes, and their worship took strange forms unauthorized by the original rules of the order. How many, if any, of these forms were the result of Indian influence is a moot question. The Penitentes turned more and more toward a primitive worship of pain and death.[2] During the period from 1800 to 1850 the order

[1] Cf. Alice C. Henderson, *Brothers of Light* (New York: Harcourt, Brace and Co., 1937), pp. 63-87.

[2] Harvey Ferguson, *Rio Grande* (New York: Knopf, 1933), p. 118.

established a firm hold on the Spanish-American people,
and when Bishop Lamy and the French priests arrived in
the 1850's, the local brotherhoods did not care to relinquish their power, particularly to foreign priests who were
not Franciscans. This did not please the priests, who tried
to insist on supervision of Penitente rites, particularly to
soften the savagery of the penances. As a means of coer-
cion, bishops and priests opposed the order and threatened
to deprive lodge members of the sacraments. The dis-
pleasure of Church officials did somewhat weaken the
order, but it had the more important effect of driving it
partly underground. Until this time the Penitentes had
been as open in their ceremonies as the modern Knights
of Columbus, but they now became a secret order. As
official anger increased, so did secrecy, yet it was a peculiar
form of secrecy, for as late as 1890 or 1900 far more native
Spanish Americans were Penitentes than were not.[3] The
Anglos in the territory often ridiculed the Penitente religious rites, with the result that by 1875 many of these
rites were held at night, far back in the mountains, and
intruders were gruffly warned away or threatened with
bodily violence. Rumors were still current in 1952 of persons who had disappeared because of their interference
with Penitente rites.

Although the strength of the Penitentes has been declining for 75 years, the order is by no means dead. In the
isolated villages of the Sangre de Christo Mountains,
probably half the adult males are still members. In the
larger towns and villages the percentage is much smaller
but the number is still large. Though the bulk of the
membership usually consists of small farmers and stock-
men, many persons of high office reputedly have been
Penitentes, and many reputedly still are, especially poli-

[3] Henderson, *Brothers of Light*, p. 72, and Laurence F. Lee, "Los Hermanos Penitentes" (Master's thesis, University of New Mexico, Albuquerque, New Mexico, 1910), p. 5.

ticians. The New Mexico historian, Twitchell, even in 1912 said that the order "has so degenerated that it is nothing today but an anomalous body of simple, credulous men, under the guidance of some unscrupulous politicians."[4] After almost a hundred years of opposition, the Church recently has officially recognized the Penitente Brotherhood. In San Miguel County, of which Las Vegas is the county seat, two factions fell into serious dispute, threatening the unity of the parish and the peace of the community. To resolve this dispute, Archbishop Byrnes of Santa Fe, in 1946, recognized the Penitentes as a part of the Church. Today there are Penitente lodges in most of the counties of New Mexico and southern Colorado. Their greatest strength is in the central mountain region of New Mexico, in San Miguel, Mora, Taos, Rio Arriba, Sandoval, Santa Fe, and Torrance counties. This is an area of other cultural survivals. Here, in isolated villages, one may see hand-dug and hand-cleaned irrigation ditches, the flumes of which are made of hand-hollowed logs. Here there is still fear of the Evil Eye; here the existence of witches is accepted or is a matter of serious argument; here there are roads passable only by wagon; here miracles still occur; grandfather's shed may still contain his old wooden plow or decrepit solid-wheeled cart, both kept to remind him of his youth; here goats, cattle, and horses may yet thresh by trampling the grain which was harvested with a hand sickle. Here sixteenth-century Spanish dances are still known, Spanish ballads of sixteenth-century style are still sung; here corrupted forms of miracle plays and religious pageants are a matter of village heritage, some being corrupted but recognizable forms of those in use in fifteenth-century Spain. In short, Penitente rites are by no means the only cultural survival; they are simply the one, chosen from a multitude, here discussed.

[4] R. E. Twitchell, *Leading Facts of New Mexico History* (Cedar Rapids, Iowa: The Torch Press, 1912), II, 168.

This flagellant brotherhood is now 350 years old in New Mexico; its membership has been numbered by the tens of thousands and is still numbered by the thousands, yet it is known only locally. Most encyclopedias make no mention of this unusual group. At best there is a very brief statement—one major encyclopedia, for example, devotes one sentence to it which contains two errors of fact: that the members are converted Indians, and that the order had died out by 1900. This lack of knowledge is not very surprising, for a generation or two ago the punishment for a member who violated the secrecy of the order was serious, reputedly including burial alive. In more recent years this secrecy has been somewhat less pronounced. One *Hermano Mayor* even permitted documentary films to be made; though expelled from the order, he was not physically punished. Other *Hermanos Mayores* have permitted photographs of processions and even of crucifixions, without, so far as the author knows, any serious consequences to themselves. Yet even today an outsider is not welcome, and as late as 1948 one of the *compañeros* at a procession carried a rifle. Much of this exclusiveness is due to the *Americanos* who go "Penitente hunting" at Easter, shining bright car lights on any chance procession. Such persons may receive a rock through the windshield; but if ones goes ahead of time to make preparation, preferably through a local intermediary, courtesy is met with courtesy, and that which is public for the village as a whole may be seen without molestation.

The Penitente brotherhood is a basically religious order whose members are all Catholics. It performs useful but secular social, psychological, social welfare, and religious functions which will not concern us here. The order follows rather closely the pattern found by Gist in other secret societies, which he says are likely to be based on mutual aid and brotherhood, patriotism, race or nation-

ality, religion, sexual morality, temperance, and social re-
form.[5]   Other than the Easter rites, later described, there
may be a ceremony on the day of the patron saint of the
local unit.   On that day the members of one cell, with
which the author is slightly acquainted, reputedly make a
pilgrimage on their knees to a mountain shrine over a mile
away.   For about a century and a half each local lodge has
run its own affairs as it saw fit, limited only by a broad,
traditional constitution.   Many minor variations exist between lodges and within the same lodge from time to time
as it comes under the influence of succeeding *Hermanos
Mayores* in charge.   It is the author's purpose not to re-
count these minor variations but to weave out of them a
generalized picture which will do basic justice to the order
as a whole.

Each lodge is made up only of adult males.   It has
its special meeting place, the *morada,* and sometimes has
several of these chapels.   The *morada* is found in more
mountain villages than not; it varies in size depending on
the financial condition of the local unit, and varies in loca-
ton depending on the desire for secrecy of the group.
Usually it is built of adobe and consists of one large room
(the chapel) and a small room in which the secret sessions
are held and where the whips, chains, and other parapher-
nalia are kept.   There are one or two small, high windows.
The chapel has an altar or platform and a few benches.
Some villages have one *morada* in the village and another
back in the mountains near "Calvary."   Chimayo, one of
the current strongholds, has at least half a dozen *moradas*.
Women, children, and visitors are on occasion welcomed
to the chapel, but never into the inner room.   It was reported to the author that in one small, isolated village the
morada was a sort of lean-to against the village church,

[5] Noel P. Gist, "Dogma and Doctrine in Secret Societies," *Sociology and
Social Research,* XXIII (Nov., 1938), 121-30.

and that the church was used as the Penitente chapel. If true, this is unusual, for priests have been forbidden for the last 100 years to hold mass in a Penitente chapel.

The officials of a typical Penitente lodge,[6] all elected, include: (1) *Hermano Mayor* ("Older Brother"), who is the head of the organization and has general oversight— he is the superior officer to whom members may turn in time of trouble or when disputes occur; (2) *Celador* ("Warden"), who serves as the caretaker of the *morada* and as sergeant-at-arms; (3) *Coadjutor* ("Helper"), who cleanses the scourges and the bodies of the penitents after flagellation; (4) *Infermero* ("Nurse"), who looks after the sick members and does other works of mercy and charity; (5) *Mandatario* ("Collector"), who is treasurer; (6) *Maestro de Novios* ("Teacher of Novices"), who examines new members and instructs them in their obligations; (7) *Secretario* ("Secretary"), who is the custodian of the book of rules, and explains the rules to the members; (8) *Sangrador* ("Bloodletter"), who inflicts the seal of the Penitentes, three horizontal and three vertical gashes across the back, cut with a flint or glass knife—he may occasionally whip members as punishment; (9) *Resador* ("Praying One"), who reads from the handwritten ritual book, praying for the flagellants during their penance—he also takes a major part in some of the nonflagellation ceremonies; (10) *Pitero* ("Flute player"), who, during the ceremonies and marches, plays on a wooden flute, furnishing all the music except that from the *metracas*, a ratchet type of rattle, if the noise they make may be considered music. As a whole these officers are called *Los Hermanos de Luz* ("Brothers of Light"). Theoretically one must have whipped himself five years to be eligible for officership, but it is rather reliably reported

[6] This material was drawn from a number of sources, but follows the order given in Lee, "Los Hermanos Penitentes," pp. 7-9.

that this rule is now adhered to only in the selection of the *Hermanos Mayores*. After five years of flagellation, the member scourges himself only if he wishes to do special penance.

The most significant and interesting pattern of Penitente ceremonies occurs during Holy Week.[7] On Holy Tuesday night the ceremonies begin. Each Penitente who will participate goes to the door of the *morada* and the officers inside ask ritual questions and receive ritual answers. The Penitente then enters and receives "the thing of obligation"—the six gashes. He then ritually asks for and receives blows of the lash for the three meditations of the passion of the Lord, the five wounds of Christ, the Seven Last Words, and the forty days in the wilderness. Usually he faints before he has fully received the forty strokes for the forty days in the wilderness. He is cared for by the *Coadjutor* and may or may not be taken to his home. Ash Wednesday is occupied with confession, prayer, ceremonial processions to the cemetery cross, and, in earlier days, additional ceremonies, and in some villages the procession of the *Carreta del Muerto*—a heavy, home-made cart. In the cart rides a hand-carved, skeleton-like effigy of death, holding a drawn bow and arrow. The cart is drawn by men harnessed by their necks or in other ways so as to make this penitential task extremely difficult. If not previously done, Christ is now chosen, by miracle, by lot, or by election. Some, but not extreme, honor is attached to serving as the *Cristo;* he is usually not over middle age, and the same person is not chosen twice. Late

[7] The following material is drawn from Lee, "Los Hermanos Penitentes," pp. 10-20; Henderson, *Brothers of Light*, pp. 25-81; Charles F. Lummis, *The Land of Poco Tiempo* (New York: Charles Scribner's Sons, 1897), chap. ii; Alice Marriot, *Maria: The Potter of San Ildefonso* (Norman, Oklahoma: University of Oklahoma Press, 1948), chap. v; and numerous verbal eye-witness accounts and talks with Penitentes by the author. Because of the wide agreement of these sources, there is no attempt to make more specific citations.

Thursday night a formal procession is made to "Calvary."
At the head of the procession is usually a statue of Christ
and/or *santos*—locally carved saints. Next come the
chosen *Cristo,* carrying his cross, and sometimes others,
also carrying crosses. All the officers are present, the
Pitero playing his flute, the *Rezador* praying, and all
chanting more or less in unison. A typical chant is:

> Penitence, penitence,
> Sin no more, unfortunate man,
> Examine your conscience.
> Come to the temple and hear the Voice.
>
> It is time to make penance,
> You who have been too busy;
> Take warning and repent,
> Examine your conscience.[8]

Those actively engaged in self-flagellation are accompanied
by *compañeros* who carry lanterns, help those who fall,
and generally lend both moral and physical support to the
ceremony.

Those who are actually engaged in flagellation occasionally wear black coverings over their heads to keep their
identities secret. The whips are usually of a type of yucca
locally called *amole* and Spanish Dagger. The whips are
about three feet long, four inches wide, and an inch thick,
with the fibers pounded until they resemble hemp. Sometimes bits of glass or wire are tied on, and leather whips
are sometimes used. Usually one or more Penitentes, instead of scourging themselves, will make the journey with
sharp cactus bound tightly to their bare backs and chests,
dragging chains on their ankles. Thorns of various types
are also used. Although different steps are used, it is
common for the Penitente to take a few steps, swing the
whip over one shoulder, take a few more, and swing it over

[8] Translated by Henderson, *Los Hermanos Penitentes,* p. 36.

the other shoulder. Before long, blood spatters at every
stroke and so stains the trousers that it appears that the
legs, too, are bleeding.

This procession usually goes either to the mountain
morada or to the "Calvary," and then before daylight re-
turns to the *morada* near the village. On Friday morning
further ceremonies and processions occur, usually including
one to the big cross in the cemetery, during which march
there may or may not be further flagellation. A service is
then held in the chapel, with hymns, chants, and prayers.
That afternoon another march usually occurs, either to
"Calvary," to the cemetery again, or to a neighboring
morada. In the old days it was this march which ended
in the crucifixion, but for many years this final ceremony
has occurred only at night. This night procession is typically the most barbaric of all, with the *Cristo* again strug-
gling under his cross, and with brutal scourging of already
lacerated backs. When Calvary is reached, the *Cristo*
(now more often an effigy) is tightly lashed to the cross.
In the old days he was nailed, and his side slashed. The
cross is placed in a hole and a sermon on the Seven Last
Words is read. The *Cristo* stays on the cross until he
faints, usually within half an hour or so. He is immediately taken down and removed to the *morada* and cared
for by the *coadjutor*. In the old days *Cristos* sometimes
died, as did flagellants. The author heard several reports
of such an occurrence within the past ten years, as well as
reports of the reintroduction of the use of nails, but none
of these reports could be traced closely enough to be considered more than rumor.

After the crucifixion scene, the Penitentes return to the
morada to rest briefly. Late Friday night or Saturday
morning the whole populace gathers at the church or the
Penitente chapel for the *tinieblas* ("earthquake"). The
church is darkened except for 12 or 24 candles. After a

hymn, 12 psalms are read and the candles are extinguished. Each extinguishment signifies the departure of a disciple from the Lord. After the end of the last psalm, the church is in darkness, and the Biblically recorded earthquake is re-enacted by the clanking of chains, beating on tin, the racket of *metracas*, the shrieks of women, and the slap of Penitente whips. This lasts for about five minues. Someone then calls for a prayer for a loved one in purgatory, and the *tinieblas* and lashing are repeated for each prayer that is asked. At the end, the Penitentes return to the *morada* to elect officers for the next year, and then return home.

As of 1953, the Penitentes still exist, and though the old rites are still carried out, they are more rare and the processions are shorter and less frequent. The brotherhood still is a religious society and still has a significant political power, but rapid cultural change stemming from the deisolation of villages is doing what opposition by the Church and state was unable fully to accomplish in a hundred years. Within a generation it is probable that Penitente processions, at least with scourging, will be a matter of cultural history only.

BIBLIOGRAPHY

Altus, William D. "The American Mexican: The Survival of a Culture," *Journal of Social Psychology*, XXIX (May, 1949), 211-20.

Anthony, Donald E. "Filipino Labor in Central California," *Sociology and Social Research*, XVI (Nov.-Dec., 1931), 149-56.

Bauken, Manuel. *I Have Lived with the American People.* Caldwell, Idaho: Caxton Printers, 1948.

———. "Our Fighting Love for Freedom: 1200 Members of the First Filipino Infantry Take Oath of Allegiance which Makes Them Citizens," *Asia*, XLIII (June, 1943), 347-59.

———. "Where Is the Heart of America?" *New Republic*, CIII (Sept. 23, 1940), 410.

———. "You Can't Marry a Filipino," *Commonweal*, XLI (March 16, 1945), 534-37.

Begeman, Jean. "Wetbacks—Slaves of Today," *New Republic*, CXXVI (March 10, 1952), 15-16.

Berne, Eric. "Cultural Aspects of a Multiple Murder," *Psychiatric Quarterly (Supplement)*, XXIV (1950), 250-69.

Berry, Brewton. *Race Relations.* Boston: Houghton-Mifflin, 1951.

Block, Louis. *Facts about Filipino Immigration to California.* Sacramento, California: Department of Industrial Relations, 1930 (Special Bulletin No. 3).

Bogardus, E. S. "Mexican-American Youth and Gangs," *Sociology and Social Research*, XXVIII (Sept., 1943), 55-66.

———. *The Mexican in the United States.* Los Angeles: University of Southern California Press, 1934.

———. "The Filipino Press in the United States," *Sociology and Social Research*, XVIII (July-Aug., 1933), 581-85.

———. "What Race Are Filipinos?" *Sociology and Social Research*, XVI (Jan.-Feb., 1932), 274-79.

———. "The Filipino Immigrant Problem," *Sociology and Social Research*, XIII (May-June, 1929), 472-79.

———. "American Attitudes toward Filipinos," *Sociology and Social Research*, XIV (Sept.-Oct., 1929), 56-69.

———. "Filipino Immigrant Attitudes," *Sociology and Social Research*, XIV (May-June, 1930), 469-79.

Border Trends. Southwest Area Office, Unitarian Service Committee, October, 1948.

Bright, Robert. *The Life and Death of Little Jo.* New York: Doubleday-Doran and Co., 1944.

Broom, Leonard, and Eshref Shevsky. "Mexicans in the United States: A Problem in Social Differentiation," *Sociology and Social Research*, XXXVI (Jan.-Feb., 1952), 150-58.

Brown, F. J., and J. S. Roucek. *One America.* New York: Prentice-Hall, 1945.

Brown, Malcolm, and Orin Cassmore. *Migratory Cotton Pickers in Arizona.* Washington: Government Printing Office, 1939.

Brown, Warren. "The Communal and Individual Personality Structure of the Puerto Rican in New York." Address delivered before the American Anthropological Association, New York, 1949.

Burma, John H. "The Background of the Current Situation for Filipino-Americans," *Social Forces*, XXX (Oct., 1951), 42-48.

———. "The Present Status of the Spanish Americans of New Mexico," *Social Forces*, XXVIII (Dec., 1949), 133-38.

Cabranes, Manuel. *Progress Report on the Puerto Rican Migrants.* New York: Puerto Rico Department of Labor, 1950.

Carlson, Hilding B., and Norma Henderson. "The Intelligence

of American Children of Mexican Parentage," *Journal of Abnormal and Social Psychology*, XLV (July, 1950), 544-51.

Carter, Hugh, and Bernice Doster. "Social Characteristics of Aliens from the Southwest Registered for Selective Service during World War II," *Immigration and Naturalization Service Monthly Review*, VIII (1951), 88-94.

Catapusan, B. T. "The Filipino's Social Adjustment in the United States." Unpublished Ph.D. dissertation, University of Southern California, 1940.

————. "Problems of Filipino Students in America," *Sociology and Social Research*, XXVI (Nov., 1941), 146-53.

————. "Leisure Time Problems of Filipino Immigrants," *Sociology and Social Research*, XXIV (July, 1940), 541-49.

————. "Filipino Immigrants and Public Relief in the United States," *Sociology and Social Research*, XXIII (July-Aug., 1939), 546-54.

————. "Filipino Intermarriage Problems in the United States," *Sociology and Social Research*, XXII (Jan., 1938), 265-72.

————. "The Filipino Labor Cycles in the United States," *Sociology and Social Research*, XIX (Sept., 1934), 61-63.

Chambers, R. L. "The New Mexico Pattern," *Common Ground*, X (Summer, 1949), 20-27.

Chenault, Lawrence R. *The Puerto Rican Migrant in New York City*. New York: Columbia University Press, 1938.

Columbia University, Bureau of Applied Social Research. *The Puerto Ricans of New York City*. New York: Puerto Rico Department of Labor, 1948.

Cooke, W. Henry. "The Segregation of Mexican-American School Children in Southern California," *School and Society*, LXVII (June 5, 1948), 417-21.

Corpus, S. F. "Second Generation Filipinos in Los Angeles," *Sociology and Social Research*, XXII (May, 1938), 446-51.

Crain, Forest Burr. "The Occupational Distribution of Spanish-Name People in Austin, Texas." Unpublished Master's thesis, University of Texas, 1948.

Crasilneck, Harold B. "A Study of One Hundred Male Latin-American Juvenile Delinquents in San Antonio, Texas." Unpublished Master's thesis. University of Texas, 1948.

Crawford, W. Rex. "The Latin-American in Wartime United States," *Annals of the American Academy of Political and Social Science,* CCXXIII (Sept., 1942), 123-31.

Fairchild, Henry Pratt. *Greek Immigration to the United States.* New Haven, Connecticut: Yale University Press, 1911.

Federal Interagency Committee on Migrant Labor. *Migrant Labor . . . A Human Problem.* Washington: U. S. Department of Agriculture, 1947.

Fergusson, Harvey. *Rio Grande.* New York: Knopf and Co., 1933.

Feria, R. T. "War and Status of Filipino Immigrants," *Sociology and Social Research,* XXXI (Sept.-Oct., 1946), 48-53.

Fogartie, Ruth Ann. *Texas-Born Spanish-Name Students in Texas Colleges and Universities (1936-46)* (Inter-American Education Occasional Papers, III). Austin, Texas: University of Texas Press, 1948.

Foster, N. "The Legal Status of Filipino Intermarriages in California," *Sociology and Social Research,* XVIII (May-June, 1933), 441-54.

Gamio, Manuel. *Mexican Immigration to the United States.* Chicago: University of Chicago Press, 1930.

———. *The Mexican Immigrant: His Life Story.* Chicago: University of Chicago Press, 1930.

Garner, Claud. *Wet Back.* New York: Coward-McCann, 1947.

Gist, Noel P. "Dogma and Doctrine in Secret Societies," *Sociology and Social Research,* XXIII (Nov., 1938), 121-30.

Goldstein, Marcus S. *Demographic and Bodily Changes in Descendants of Mexican Immigrants.* Austin, Texas: Institute of Latin American Studies, 1943.

Gonzalo, D. F. "Social Adjustments of Filipinos in America," *Sociology and Social Research,* XXXIV (Nov.-Dec., 1949), 166-73.

Governor's Interracial Commission of Minnesota. *The Mexican in Minnesota.* St. Paul, Minnesota: State of Minnesota, 1948.

Griffith, Beatrice W. *American Me.* Boston: Houghton-Mifflin, 1948.

———. "Viva Roybal—Viva America," *Common Ground,* X (Aug., 1949), 61-70.

Handman, Max. "San Antonio," *Survey*, LXVI (May 1, 1931), 163-66.

———. "Economic Reasons for the Coming of the Mexican Immigrant," *American Journal of Sociology*, XXXV (Jan., 1930), 601-11.

Harper, Allen G., Andrew R. Cordova, and Kaleroo Oberg. *Man and Resources in the Middle Rio Grande Valley*. Albuquerque, New Mexico: University of New Mexico Press, 1943.

Harvey, Louise F. "The Delinquent Mexican Boy," *Journal of Educational Research*, XLII (April, 1949), 573-85.

Hazard, C. E. *Welfare of Families of Sugar Beet Laborers* (Children's Bureau Publication, No. 247). Washington: United States Department of Labor, 1939.

Hayner, Norman S. "Social Factors in Oriental Crime," *American Journal of Sociology*, XLIII (May, 1938), 908-19.

Henderson, Alice C. *Brothers of Light*. New York: Harcourt, Brace and Co., 1937.

Hill, George W. *Texas-Mexican Migratory Agricultural Workers in Wisconsin*. Madison, Wisconsin: Agricultural Experiment Station, University of Wisconsin, 1948.

Hughes, Marie M. "Southern California's Educational and Community Projects Related to Latin Americans," Conference on the Problems of Education among Spanish-Speaking Populations of Our Southwest, August 19-24, 1943.

Humphrey, Norman D. "The Changing Structure of the Detroit Mexican Family: An Index of Acculturation," *American Sociological Review*, IX (Dec., 1944), 622-26.

———. "The Cultural Background of the Mexican Immigrant," *Rural Sociology*, XIII (1948), 239-55.

Interpreter Releases, XX, Series C, No. 37, Oct. 13, 1943.

Johnson, Dallas. "They Fenced Tolerance In," *Survey Graphic*, XXXVI (July, 1947), 398-99.

Johnson, Elizabeth S. *Welfare of Families of Sugar Beet Laborers* (Children's Bureau Publication, No. 247). Washington: United States Department of Labor, 1939.

Jones, Robert C. "Ethnic Family Patterns: The Mexican Family in the United States," *American Journal of Sociology*, LIII (May, 1948), 450-52.

————. "Mexican American Youth," *Sociology and Social Research*, XXXII (March-April, 1948), 793-97.

Kaufman, Charles. *Fiesta in Manhattan*. New York: Morrow, 1939.

Kibbee, Pauline R. "The American Standard—For All Americans," *Common Ground*, X (Autumn, 1949), 19-27.

————. *Latin Americans in Texas*. Albuquerque, New Mexico: University of New Mexico Press, 1946.

Kihss, Peter. *Puerto Rico and Us: Three Articles from the New York "Times."* New York: Department of Labor of Puerto Rico, Migration Division, 1953.

Kirk, Grayson. "Filipinos," *Annals of the American Academy of Political and Social Science*, CCXXIII (Sept., 1942), 45-48.

Lasker, Bruno. *Filipino Immigration*. Chicago: University of Chicago Press, 1931.

Laughlin, Ruth. "Coronado's Country and Its People," *Survey Graphic*, XXIX (May, 1940), 277-82.

Lee, Laurence F. "Los Hermanos Penitentes." Unpublished Master's thesis, University of New Mexico, 1910.

Lemert, E. M., and Judy Rosberg. "Crime and Punishment among Minority Groups in Los Angeles County," *Proceedings of the Pacific Coast Sociological Society*, June, 1946.

Leonard, Olen, and C. P. Loomis. *The Culture of a Contemporarary Rural Community: El Cerrito, New Mexico* (Rural Life Studies, No. 1). Washington: United States Department of Agriculture, 1941.

Liebson, Art. "The Wetback Invasion," *Common Ground*, X (Autumn, 1949), pp. 11-19.

Little, Wilson. *Spanish Speaking Children in Texas*. Austin, Texas: University of Texas Press, 1944.

Loomis, C. P. "Informal Groupings in a Spanish American Village," *Sociometry*, IV (Feb., 1941), 40-51.

Lummis, Charles F. *The Land of Poco Tiempo*. New York: Charles Scribner's Sons, 1897.

McDonogh, Edward C. "Status Levels of Mexicans," *Sociology and Social Research*, XXXV (Nov.-Dec., 1950), 449-59.

————. "Status Levels of the American Jews," *Sociology and Social Research*, XXXII (July-Aug., 1948), 944-53.

McWilliams, Carey. *Brothers under the Skin*. Boston: Little, Brown, and Co., 1943.
————. "California and the Wetback," *Common Ground*, (Summer, 1949), pp. 15-20.
————. "Exit—the Filipino," *Nation*, CXLI (Sept. 4, 1935), 265.
————. *Factories in the Field*. Boston: Little, Brown, and Co., 1939.
————. *Ill Fares the Land*. Boston: Little, Brown, and Co., 1942.
————. *North from Mexico*. New York: Lippincott, 1949.
————. "Thirty-six Thousand New Aliens in California," *Pacific Weekly* (Aug. 24, 1936), pp. 119 ff.
Manuel, Herschel T. *The Education of Mexican and Spanish-Speaking Children in Texas*. Austin, Texas: The Fund for Research in the Social Sciences, University of Texas, 1930.
Marden, Charles F. *Minorities in American Society*. New York: American Book Company, 1952.
Menefee, Selden C. *Mexican Migratory Workers in South Texas*. Washington: Government Printing Office, 1941.
————, and Orin C. Cassmore. *The Pecan Shellers of San Antonio*. Washington: Government Printing Office, 1940.
Mexican Fact Finding Committee. *Mexicans in California*. Sacramento, California: State Printing Office, 1930.
Meyers, Frederic. *Spanish-Name Persons in the Labor Force in Manufacturing Industry in Texas* (Inter-American Occasional Papers, VIII). Austin, Texas: University of Texas Press, 1951.
Miller, Watson B. "Administering Our Immigration Laws," *Annals of the American Academy of Political and Social Science*, CCLXII (March, 1949), 178-84.
Mills, C. Wright, Clarence Senior, and Rose Goldsen. *The Puerto Rican Journey*. New York: Harper and Brothers, 1950.
Moody, Alan. *Sleep in the Sun*. Boston: Houghton-Mifflin Co., 1945.
National Opinion Research Center. *The Spanish-Speaking Population of Denver—Housing, Employment, Health, Recreation, Education*. Denver, Colorado: Denver Unity Council, 1946.

Nelson, Eastin, and Frederic Meyers. *Labor Requirements and Labor Resources in the Lower Rio Grande Valley of Texas* (Inter-American Occasional Papers, VI). Austin, Texas, University of Texas Press, 1950.

New York City Mayor's Committee on Puerto Rican Affairs. *The Puerto Rican Pupils in the Public Schools of New York City.* New York: The Committee, 1951.

Nunn, Guy T. *White Shadows.* New York: Reynal and Hitchcock, 1947.

Pagano, Jo. *The Paesanos.* Boston: Little, Brown, and Co., 1940.

Panunzio, Constantine. *How Mexicans Earn and Live.* Berkeley, California: University of California Press, 1933.

Pasamanick, Benjamin. "The Intelligence of American Children of Mexican Parentage: A Discussion of Uncontrolled Variables," *Journal of Abnormal and Social Psychology*, XLVI (Oct., 1951), 598-602.

Pattee, Richard. "The Puerto Ricans," *Annals of the American Academy of Political and Social Science*, CCXXIII (Sept., 1942), 49-54.

Phillips, Lester H. "Segregation in Education: A California Case Study," *Phylon*, X (Fourth Quarter, 1949), 407-13.

Paz, Frank X. *Mexican-Americans in Chicago.* Chicago: Chicago Council of Social Agencies, 1948.

President's Commission on Migratory Labor. *Migratory Labor in American Agriculture.* Washington: Government Printing Office, 1951.

————. *Report of the President's Commission on Migratory Labor.* Washington: Government Printing Office, 1951.

Report on Crime and the Foreign Born. Washington: Government Printing Office, 1931.

Reynolds, Annie. *The Education of Spanish-Speaking Children in Five Southwestern States.* Washington: United States Department of the Interior, 1933.

Roberts, Marta. *Tumbleweed.* New York: Putnam's, 1940.

Rojo, T. A. "Social Maladjustment among Filipinos in the United States," *Sociology and Social Research*, XXI (May, 1937), 447-57.

Rose, Arnold (ed.). *Race Prejudice and Discrimination.* New York: Knopf, 1948.

————, and Caroline Rose. *America Divided.* New York: Knopf, 1948.

Sanchez, George I. *Concerning Segregation of Spanish-Speaking Children in the Public Schools* (Inter-American Occasional Papers, IX). Austin, Texas: University of Texas Press, 1951.

————. *Forgotten People.* Albuquerque, New Mexico: University of New Mexico Press, 1940.

————, and Lyle Saunders. *Wetbacks* (A Preliminary Report to the Advisory Committee, Study of Spanish-Speaking People). Austin, Texas: University of Texas Press, 1949.

Santos, A. P. "A Filipino Race in the Making," *Sociology and Social Research,* XXIV (Nov., 1939), 158-62.

Saunders, Lyle. *The Spanish-Speaking Population of Texas* (Inter-American Education Occasional Papers, V). Austin, Texas: University of Texas Papers, 1949.

————, and Olen E. Leonard. *The Wetback in the Lower Rio Grande Valley of Texas* (Inter-American Education Occasional Papers, VII). Austin, Texas: University of Texas Press, 1951.

Schermerhorn, R. A. *These Our People.* Boston: D. C. Heath, 1949.

Schepses, Erwin. "Puerto Rican Delinquent Boys in New York City," *Social Service Review,* XXIII (March, 1949), 51-56.

Schorr, Daniel L. " 'Re-Converting' Mexican Americans," *New Republic,* CXV (Sept. 30, 1946), 412-13.

Senior, Clarence. *Puerto Rican Emigration.* Rio Piedras, Puerto Rico: University of Puerto Rico, 1947.

Senter, Donovan, and Florence Hawley. "The Grammar School as the Basic Acculturating Influence for Native New Mexicans," *Social Forces,* XXIV (May, 1946), 398-407.

Sininger, Harlan. "New Mexico's Reading Survey." Unpublished Master's thesis, University of New Mexico, 1930.

Sixteenth Census of the United States: 1940. *Population of Spanish Mother Tongue: 1940.* Series P-15, No. 1, June, 1942.

Smith, T. Lynn. *The Sociology of Rural Life.* New York: Harper and Bros., 1947.

Stegner, Wallace. *One Nation*. Boston: Houghton-Mifflin, 1945.

Stillwell, Hart. *Border City*. New York: Doubleday-Doran, 1945.

————. "The Wetback Tide," *Common Ground*, X (Summer, 1949), 3-14.

Taylor, M. C. "Retardation of Mexican Children in Albuquerque Schools." Unpublished Master's thesis, Stanford University, 1927.

Taylor, Paul S. *An American-Mexican Frontier: Neuces County, Texas*. Chapel Hill, North Carolina: University of North Carolina Press, 1934.

————. *Mexican Labor in the United States*, IV. Berkeley, California: University of California Press, 1932.

————. "Mexicans North of the Rio Grande," *Survey*, LXVI (May 1, 1931), 135-40.

Thomas, Howard E., and Florence Taylor. *Migrant Farm Labor in Colorado: A Study of Migratory Families*. New York: National Child Labor Committee, 1951.

Tireman, Lloyd S. *Teaching Spanish-Speaking Children*. Albuquerque, New Mexico: University of New Mexico Press, 1948.

Tuck, Ruth D. *Not with the Fist*. New York: Harcourt, Brace and Co., 1946.

Twitchell, R. E. *Leading Facts of New Mexico History*. Cedar Rapids, Iowa: The Torch Press, 1912.

Uniform Crime Reports, Vol. X (1939), No. 4; Vol. XI (1940), No. 4; Vol. XII (1941), No. 4. Washington: Department of Justice.

"Vital Statistics in New Mexico," *New Mexico Health Officer*, X (July, 1942), 4-6.

Warburton, Amber A., Helen Wood, and Marian M. Crane. *The Work and Welfare of Agricultural Laborers in Hildalgo County, Texas* (Children's Bureau Publication, 298). Washington: United States Department of Labor, 1943.

Weeks, Oliver D. "The Texas-Mexican and the Politics of South Texas," *American Political Science Review*, XXIV (Aug., 1930), 606-27.

Weinberg, George. "School in Transition," *Journal of Educational Sociology*, XXV (Nov., 1951), 140-45.

Welfare Council of New York City. *Puerto Ricans in New York City*. New York: The Council, 1948.

Wheeler, Helen. "The Puerto Rican Population of New York, New York," *Sociology and Social Research*, XXXV (Nov.-Dec., 1950), 123-27.

Wilson, Frank E. "El Cerrito: A Changing Culture." Unpublished Master's thesis, New Mexico Highlands University, 1949.

Woofter, T. J. *Races and Ethnics Groups in American Life*. New York: McGraw-Hill, 1933.

Yarbrough, C. L. "Age-Grade Status of Texas Children of Latin American Descent," *Journal of Educational Research*, XL (Sept., 1946), 14-27.

Young, Donald R. *American Minority Peoples*. New York: Harper and Bros., 1932.

INDEX